Fast&Easy
earrings

Kalmbach Books

21027 Crossroads Circle

Waukesha, Wisconsin 53186

www.JewelryandBeadingStore.com

Published in 2015

19 18 17 16 15   1 2 3 4 5

Manufactured in China

ISBN: 978-1-62700-241-7

EISBN: 978-1-62700-242-4

The material in this book has appeared previously in *Bead Style* magazine. *Bead Style* is registered as a trademark.

Editor: Erica Swanson

Book Design: Carole Ross

Illustrator: Kellie Jaeger

Photographers: William Zuback and James Forbes

Library of Congress Control Number: 2014958390

Fast & Easy
earrings

Erica Swanson

Waukesha, Wisconsin

Contents

p.16

p.17

p.37

p.39

Stones

Pearls

Mixed Materials

Contributors............... 110

Introduction

Welcome to boundless possibilities!

Earrings are a wonderful way to express your style. They're quick to make and easy to wear with just about anything. Earrings are the perfect accessory to top off a polished outfit or a nice way to dress up a t-shirt and pair of jeans. A stunning pair for a special occasion can show off any little black dress to perfection.

Whatever your style, you'll find countless ideas for accessorizing your look within these pages.

Maybe you like to make a bold statement: Inside you'll see plenty of big hoops and crystal-embellished sparklers. Perhaps you prefer a dainty look: Choose from post-style earrings and feminine drops. With easy-to-follow instructions and plenty of step-by-step photographs, you can complete any project with confidence. Design alternates offer even more ideas for customizing your pieces.

With so many options, you can make fast, fashionable, and fun earrings in a flash. You can even give them as gifts! They will always be the right size, and with so many options, you're sure to find something to fit everyone's taste.

Enjoy the variety and sparkle of earrings you can wear all year long. Have fun creating!

Erica Swanson
Editor, Kalmbach Books

Basic Materials

crystal and glass

Czech fire
polished

bicone

top-drilled bicone

cube

oval

drop

briolette

cone

round

flat back

lampworked

leaves

dagger

teardrop

fringe drops

seed beads

bugle

gemstone shapes

lentil

rondelle

round

oval

briolette

teardrop

chips

pearls, shells, and miscellaneous

round   teardrop   potato   button   stick   keshi

rice   coin   Lucite flowers   donut   shell

findings, spacers, and connectors

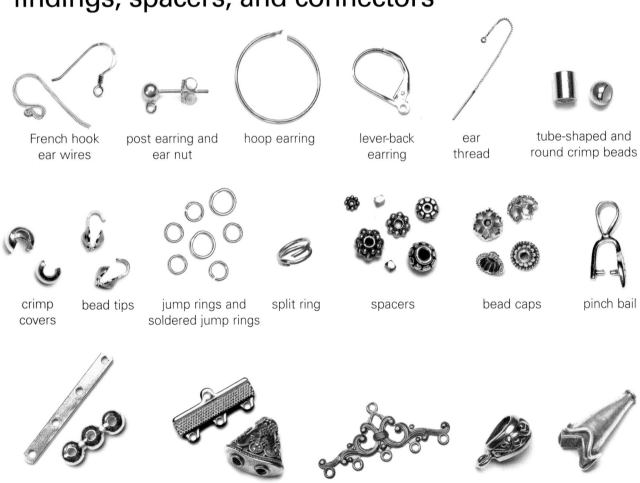

French hook ear wires   post earring and ear nut   hoop earring   lever-back earring   ear thread   tube-shaped and round crimp beads

crimp covers   bead tips   jump rings and soldered jump rings   split ring   spacers   bead caps   pinch bail

multistrand spacer bars   3-to-1 and 2-to-1 connectors   chandelier component   bail   cone

tools, materials, and chain

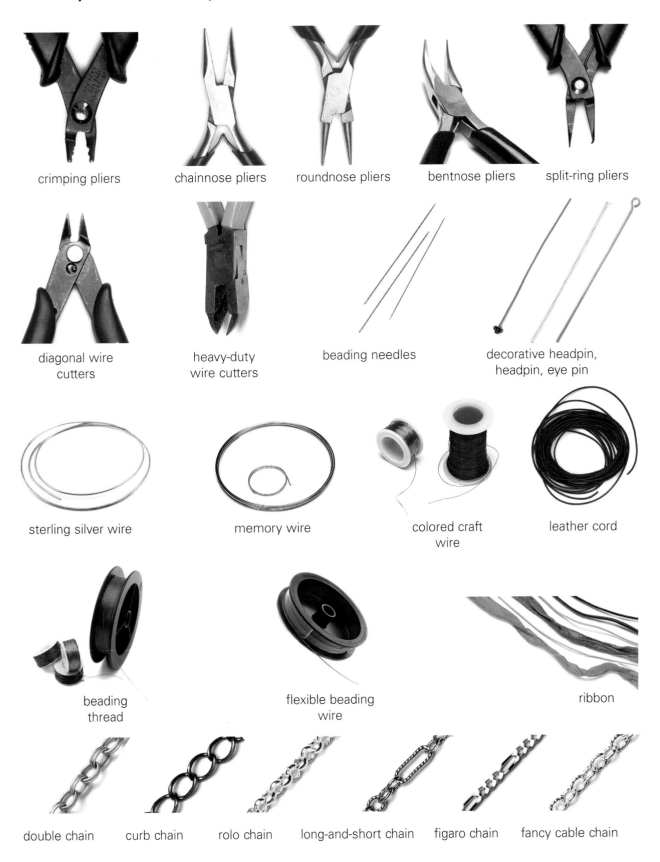

crimping pliers

chainnose pliers

roundnose pliers

bentnose pliers

split-ring pliers

diagonal wire cutters

heavy-duty wire cutters

beading needles

decorative headpin, headpin, eye pin

sterling silver wire

memory wire

colored craft wire

leather cord

beading thread

flexible beading wire

ribbon

double chain

curb chain

rolo chain

long-and-short chain

figaro chain

fancy cable chain

Basic Techniques

plain loop

1

2

3

4

Trim the wire or headpin ³⁄₈ in. (1 cm) above the top bead. Make a right-angle bend close to the bead.

Grab the wire's tip with roundnose pliers. The tip of the wire should be flush with the pliers. Roll the wire to form a half circle. Release the wire.

Reposition the pliers in the loop and continue rolling.

The finished loop should form a centered circle above the bead.

wrapped loop

1

2

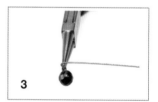

3

4

Make sure you have at least 1¼ in. (3.2 cm) of wire above the bead. With the tip of your chainnose pliers, grasp the wire directly above the bead. Bend the wire (above the pliers) into a right angle.

Using roundnose pliers, position the jaws in the bend.

Bring the wire over the top jaw of the roundnose pliers.

Reposition the pliers' lower jaw snugly into the loop. Curve the wire downward around the roundnose pliers. This is the first half of a wrapped loop.

opening and closing loops or jump rings

5

6

1

2

Position the chainnose pliers' jaws across the loop.

Wrap the wire tail around the wire stem, covering the stem between the loop and the top bead. Trim the excess wire and press the cut end close to the wraps with chainnose pliers.

Hold the loop or jump ring with two pairs of chainnose pliers or chainnose and roundnose pliers, as shown.

To open the loop or jump ring, bring one pair of pliers toward you and push the other pair away. String materials on the open loop or jump ring. Reverse the steps to close the open loop or jump ring.

overhand knot

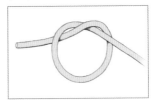

Make a loop and pass the working end through it. Pull the ends to tighten the knot.

surgeon's knot

Cross the right end over the left end and go through the loop. Go through again. Pull the ends to tighten. Cross the left end over the right end and go through once. Pull the ends to tighten.

lark's head knot

Fold a cord in half and lay it behind a ring, loop, etc. with the fold pointing down. Bring the ends through the ring from back to front, and then through the fold and tighten.

making wraps above a top-drilled bead

1

2

3

4

Center a top-drilled bead on a 3-in. (7.6 cm) piece of wire. Bend each wire upward to form a squared-off "U" shape.

Cross the wires into an "X" above the bead.

Using chainnose pliers, make a small bend in each wire to form a right angle.

Wrap the horizontal wire around the vertical wire as in a wrapped loop. Trim the excess wire.

folded crimp

1

2

3

4

Position the crimp bead in the notch closest to the crimping pliers' handle.

Separate the wires and firmly squeeze the crimp.

Move the crimp into the notch at the pliers' tip and hold the crimp as shown. Squeeze the crimp bead, folding it in half at the indentation.

Test that the folded crimp is secure.

Projects

Easy Crystal Dangles

designed by Ute Bernsen

SUPPLIES

- **4** 6 mm round crystals, in two colors
- **4** 6 mm large-hole flat spacers
- **2** 1½-in. (3.8 cm) head pins
- pair of earring wires
- chainnose and roundnose pliers
- diagonal wire cutters

1 For each earring: On a head pin, string a crystal, a spacer, and a crystal. Make the first half of a wrapped loop (Basics).

2 Attach a spacer and complete the wraps. Open the loop of an earring wire (Basics) and attach the dangle. Close the loop.

Diamond Drops

designed by Karen Karon

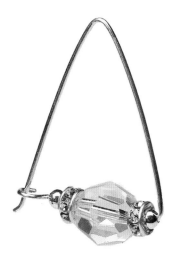

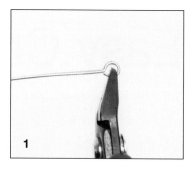

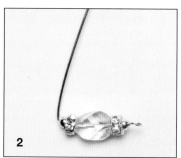

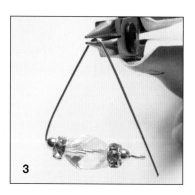

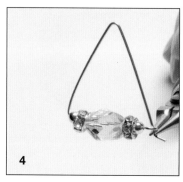

SUPPLIES

- **2** 10–14 mm crystals
- **4** 5–7 mm crystal rondelles
- **4** 3–4 mm spacers
- **8** in. (20 cm) 20-gauge
- half-hard wire
- roundnose pliers
- diagonal wire cutters
- metal file or emery board

1 Cut a 4-in. (10 cm) piece of wire. Make a plain loop (Basics). Trim the loop to make a C-shaped hook.

2 String a spacer, rondelle, crystal, rondelle, and spacer. Holding the C facing away from you, make a 45-degree bend.

3 Place your roundnose pliers 1¼ in. (3.2 cm) from the first bend. Pull the wire down to form a triangle.

4 Hook the wire in the C. Use the tip of your pliers to make a slight bend. Trim the wire and file the ends. Make a second earring.

Emerald Dangles

designed by Jane Konkel

SUPPLIES

- **2** 11 mm bead caps, with six loops
- **12** 9 mm crystal drops
- **4** 6 mm crystal margaritas
- **12** 3 mm bicone crystals
- **14** 4 mm spacers
- **72** 4 mm jump rings
- pair of earring wires
- chainnose and roundnose pliers

1 On a head pin, string a bicone crystal, a spacer, and a crystal drop. Make a wrapped loop (Basics). Make six bead units.

2 Open a jump ring (Basics) and attach a bead unit. Close the jump ring. Attach another jump ring. Make four more dangles: one with four jump rings, one with six jump rings, one with eight jump rings, and one with 10 jump rings.

3 Use a jump ring to attach each dangle and the loop of a bead cap.

4 On a head pin, string a crystal margarita, the bead cap, a margarita, and a spacer. Make a wrapped loop.

5 Open the loop of an earring wire (Basics) and attach the dangle. Close the loop. Make a second earring.

1

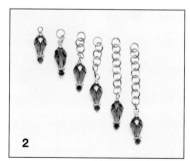

2

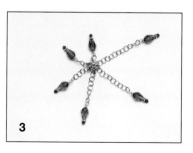

3

4

5

Crystal Clusters

designed by Beth Haywood

SUPPLIES

- **4** 8 mm faceted rondelles
- **10** 6 mm round crystals
- **20** 5 mm bicone crystals
- **4** 4 mm bicone crystals
- **4** 11º seed beads
- **30** 1½-in. (3.8 cm) head pins
- **2** 2-in. (5 cm) head pins
- pair of earring wires
- chainnose and roundnose pliers
- diagonal wire cutters

1 For each earring: On a 1½-in. (3.8 cm) head pin, string a 5 mm bicone crystal. Make a plain loop (Basics). Make 10 bicone units and five round crystal units.

2 On a 2-in. (5 cm) head pin, string: seed bead, 4 mm bicone, faceted rondelle, five bicone units, five round crystal units, five bicone units, rondelle, 4 mm bicone, and seed bead. Make a plain loop.

3 Open the loop of an earring wire (Basics). Attach the dangle and close the loop.

1

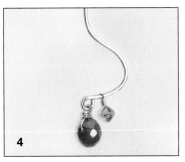

2

3

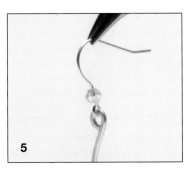

4

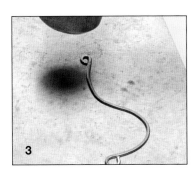

5

Winding Wire

designed by Carolina Angel

SUPPLIES

- **2** 12 mm rondelles
- **2** 6 mm bicone crystals
- **2** 4 mm bicone crystals
- 6 in. (15 cm) 20-gauge half-hard wire
- 12 in. (30 cm) 24-gauge half-hard wire
- pair of plain earring wires
- chainnose and roundnose pliers
- diagonal wire cutters
- bench block or anvil
- hammer

1 Cut a 2-in. (5 cm) piece of 24-gauge wire. String a 6 mm bicone crystal and make a set of wraps above it (Basics). Make a wrapped loop (Basics) above the wraps.

2 Cut a 4-in. (10 cm) piece of 24-gauge wire. String a rondelle and make a set of wraps above it. Make a wrapped loop. Using your fingers, wrap the wire loosely over the loop and the first set of wraps.

3 Cut a 3-in. (7.6 cm) piece of 20-gauge wire. Curve the wire as desired. Make a small loop on each end. On a bench block or anvil, hammer each side of the wire.

4 Open a loop (Basics) of the wire and attach the bicone and rondelle units. Close the loop.

5 Open the loop of an earring wire and attach the dangle. Close the loop. String a 4 mm bicone crystal on the earring wire. Make a second earring.

Tip

When hammering, lightly strike the loops. If you over-hammer, the loops may be difficult to open and close.

Blooming Filigrees

designed by Jenny Van

SUPPLIES

- **4** 16 mm double filigree flowers
- **4** 8 mm round crystals
- **2** 2-in. (5 cm) head pins
- pair of earring wires

- chainnose or bentnose pliers
- roundnose pliers
- diagonal wire cutters

1 For each earring: Using chainnose or bentnose pliers, gently bend the inner petals of a filigree flower just enough to accommodate a round crystal. Prepare a second flower.

2 On a head pin, string a crystal, two back-to-back flowers, and a crystal. Make a wrapped loop (Basics).

3 Use chainnose or bentnose pliers to close the inner petals around each crystal.

4 Open the loop of an earring wire (Basics). Attach the dangle and close the loop.

Rondelles

designed by Fernando DaSilva

SUPPLIES

- **2** 17 mm rondelles
- **2** 15 mm bead caps
- **2** 2-in. (5 cm) 20- or 22-gauge head pins
- **2** 4–6 mm jump rings
- pair of lever-back earring wires
- chainnose and roundnose pliers
- diagonal wire cutters

1 For each earring: On a head pin, string a bead cap and a rondelle. Pull the wire over the top of the rondelle.

2 Grasp the end of the wire with your roundnose pliers and roll the wire to make a loop.

3 Open a jump ring (Basics). Attach the dangle and the loop of an earring wire. Close the jump ring.

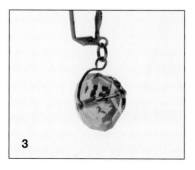

DESIGN OPTION
String a Lucite flower and a smooth rondelle for a sweet pastel pair.

Crystal Lattice

designed by Ann Cook

SUPPLIES

- **6** 4 mm bicone crystals
- **6** 13º charlottes
- **2** 41 mm kite-shaped components
- 2 in. (5 cm) cable chain, 3–4 mm links
- beading thread, size D
- **2** 4 mm jump rings
- pair of earring wires
- beading needle, size 10 or 12
- scissors
- **2** pairs of pliers
- diagonal wire cutters

Kite-shaped components from Fire Mountain Gems and Beads, firemountaingems.com.

1 For each earring: Cut a ¾-in. (1.9 cm) piece of chain. Cut a 4-in. (10 cm) piece of thread and thread a beading needle. Alternate three charlottes and three bicone crystals, then string an end link of chain. Go through the beads again. Tighten the thread to make a circle. Tie the ends together with two overhand knots (Basics). Trim the excess thread.

2 Open a jump ring (Basics). Attach the dangle and the inner loop of a kite component. Close the jump ring.

3 Open the loop of an earring wire. Attach the dangle and close the loop.

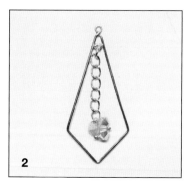

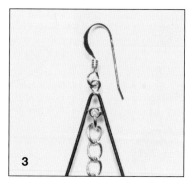

Crystallized Tourmaline

designed by Leah Hanoud

SUPPLIES

- **2** 5 mm bicone crystals
- **2** 4 mm bicone crystals
- **2** 3 mm bicone crystals
- **2** 10–12 mm diamond-shaped links
- **2** 1½ -in. (3.8 cm) head pins
- pair of earring wires
- chainnose and roundnose pliers
- diagonal wire cutters

1 On a head pin, string a 5 mm, a 4 mm, and a 3 mm bicone crystal. Using the largest part of your roundnose pliers, make the first half of a wrapped loop (Basics).

2 Attach the bead unit and a diamond-shaped link. Complete the wraps.

3 Open the loop of an earring wire (Basics). Attach the dangle and close the loop. Make a second earring.

1

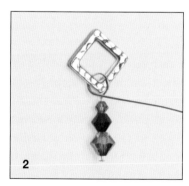

2

3

Sparkling Mesh Teardrops

designed by Becky Machinski

SUPPLIES

- **18** 4 mm bicone crystals
- 6 in. (15 cm) SilverSilk 4.8 mm eight-needle flat knitted wire
- Fireline 6 lb. test
- 9 in. (23 cm) 20- or 22-gauge wire
- 4 in. (10 cm) 26- or 28-gauge wire
- chainnose and roundnose pliers
- diagonal wire cutters
- bench block or anvil
- hammer
- needle
- pen
- metal file or emery board (optional)

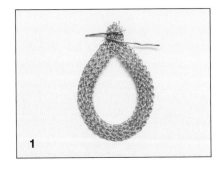

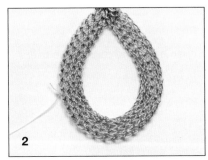

1 For each earring: Cut a 3-in. (7.6 cm) piece of knitted wire and a 2-in. (5 cm) piece of 26- or 28-gauge wire. Form a drop shape with the knitted wire. Wrap the 26- or 28-gauge wire around and through the knitted wire to secure the drop shape.

2 Cut a 12-in. (30 cm) piece of Fireline and thread it on a needle. About ¾ in. (1.9 cm) from the top of the drop, string an outer loop of the knitted wire. Tie a surgeon's knot (Basics) with the thread and trim the excess to 3 mm.

3 String nine bicone crystals, covering the 3 mm tail with the first bicone. String an outer loop of the knitted wire to secure the last bicone.

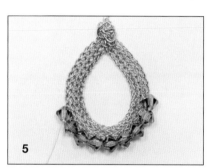

4 Go back through two or three bicones and through an outer loop of the knitted wire. Repeat until you've anchored all of the bicones.

5 Tie a knot around the knitted wire and go back through the first bicone. Trim the excess Fireline.

6 Cut a 4½-in. (11.4 cm) piece of 20- or 22-gauge wire. Use your roundnose and chainnose pliers to make a coil about ¼ in. (6 mm) in diameter.

7 On a bench block or anvil, hammer the coil.

8 Place the coil on top of the 26- or 28-gauge wrapped wire. Grasping the coil and the drop with chainnose pliers, wrap the 20- or 22-gauge wire around the drop.

9 Bend the 20- or 22-gauge wire upward so it's perpendicular to the coil.

10 Pull the wire around a pen to make an earring wire. Use pliers to bend the tip of the wire upward. Trim the excess wire and file if necessary. If desired, hammer the earring wire.

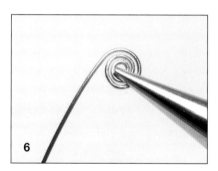

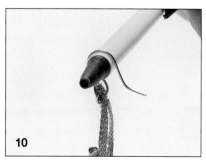

Dangle, Sparkle, and Shine

designed by Monica Lueder

SUPPLIES

- **2** 26–31 mm round pendants
- **2** 25 mm connectors
- **2** 6 mm bicone crystals
- **2** 4 mm bicone crystals
- **4** 5 mm flat-back crystals
- **6** 4 mm flat-back crystals
- **6** 3 mm flat-back crystals
- **2** 6 mm blossom bead caps

- 4 in. (10 cm) 22-gauge half-hard wire
- pair of earring wires
- chainnose and roundnose pliers
- diagonal wire cutters
- toothpick
- two-part epoxy

Brass components from Galena Beads, galenabeads.com.

1 Arrange flat-back crystals on a pendant. Mix two-part epoxy according to the package directions. Use a toothpick to apply a dot of epoxy to each flat back and the pendant. Press together and allow to dry.

2 Cut a 1-in. (2.5 cm) piece of wire. Make a plain loop (Basics). String a 4 mm bicone crystal. Make a plain loop. Cut a 1-in. (2.5 cm) piece of wire. Make a plain loop. String a 6 mm bicone crystal and a bead cap. Make a plain loop perpendicular to the first loop.

3 Open the loops (Basics) of the 4 mm bicone unit. Attach the pendant and a connector. Close the loops.

4 Open the loops of the 6 mm bicone unit. Attach the connector and an earring wire. Close the loops. Make a second earring.

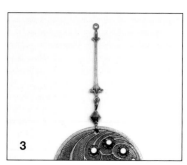

DESIGN OPTION
If you prefer shorter earrings, omit the connectors.

✳ Tip

Use isopropyl (rubbing) alcohol on a cotton swab to remove any excess epoxy before it dries.

1

2

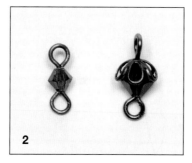

3

Crystals on a Curve

designed by Christianne Camera

SUPPLIES

- **2** 10 mm round crystals
- **8** 4 mm bicone crystals
- **10** 11º seed beads
- **10** 1½-in. (3.8 cm) head pins
- pair of earring wires with attached ring
- chainnose and roundnose pliers
- diagonal wire cutters

Earring wires with attached ring from Saki, sakisilver.com.

1 On a head pin, string a bicone crystal and an 11º seed bead. Make the first half of a wrapped loop (Basics). Make four bicone units and a round crystal unit.

2 Attach the loop of the round crystal unit and the soldered ring on an earring wire. Complete the wraps.

3 On each side of the round crystal, attach two bicone units. Complete the wraps as you go. Make a second earring.

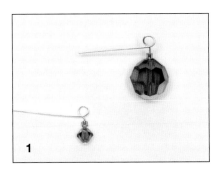

Mad for Retro Style

designed by Ashley Bunting

SUPPLIES

- **2** 10 mm margarita crystals
- **2** 13 mm round filigrees
- **2** 4 mm flat spacers
- **2** 1½ in. (3.8 cm) head pins
- pair of earring posts with cups
- pair of ear nuts
- chainnose and roundnose pliers
- diagonal wire cutters
- two-part epoxy

Earring posts from AlaCarte Clasps & WireLace, alacarteclasps.com.

1 On a head pin, string a 10 mm margarita crystal, a 13 mm filigree, and a 4 mm spacer. Make a plain loop (Basics). Continue turning the loop to snug all the elements together. Flatten the loop against the back of the filigree.
2 Mix two-part epoxy according to the package directions. Fill the cup of the earring post halfway and insert the loop of the filigree. Allow the epoxy to cure (Tip).

 Tip

Fill a small container with sugar, rice, or anything granular, and insert the earring post to keep it level while the epoxy cures.

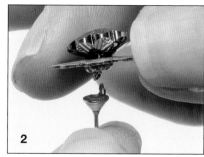

Crystallize Your Inspiration

designed by Naomi Fujimoto

SUPPLIES

BLUE EARRINGS

- **2** 20 mm cosmic crystal rings
- **2**½ in. (6.4 cm) chain, 4 mm links

COPPER EARRINGS

- **2** 18 mm de-art crystal pendants
- **2** links chain, 13 mm links, or
  2 13–15 mm jump rings
- **2** 7–8 mm jump rings

BOTH

- pair of earring wires
- **2** pairs of pliers
- diagonal wire cutters

blue earrings

1 For each earring: Cut a 1¼-in. (3.2 cm) piece of 4 mm link chain. Open the loop of an earring wire (Basics). String a cosmic ring on the chain and attach each end link and the earring wire's loop. Close the loop.

copper earrings

1 For each earring: Open a 7–8 mm jump ring (Basics). Attach a 13–15 mm jump ring or a chain link and an 18 mm pendant. Close the jump ring.

2 Open the loop of an earring wire. Attach the dangle and close the loop.

Beaded Braids

designed by Kimberly Wayne

SUPPLIES

- **2** 6 mm round crystals
- **2** 4 mm bicone crystals
- **2** 3 mm bicone crystals
- **6** 1½-in. (3.8 cm) head pins
- 4 in. (10 cm) cable chain, 2–3 mm links
- pair of earring posts with ear nuts
- chainnose and roundnose pliers
- diagonal wire cutters

1 On a head pin, string a crystal. Make a plain loop (Basics). Make three crystal units.

2 Open the loop of an earring post (Basics). Attach the end link of a chain (Tip) and close the loop.

3 Near the loop of the post, tie an overhand knot (Basics) with the chain. Do not trim the excess chain.

4 Open the loop of the round crystal unit (Basics). Attach a link of chain just below the knot and close the loop. Trim the excess chain. Attach the 4 mm bicone unit to the same link as the round unit. Attach the 3 mm bicone unit to another link. Make a second earring.

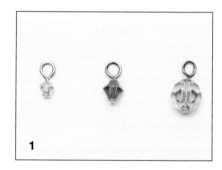

1

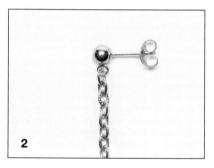

2

✿ Tip

You'll need only about an inch of chain per earring, but it's easier to start with a longer piece and knot it, attach the bead units, and then trim the excess chain. It's also easier to make the first earring and then a second to match (rather than first cutting the two pieces of chain).

3

4

Crystal Kisses

designed by Anna Elizabeth Draeger

SUPPLIES

- **16** 3 mm bicone crystals, **8** color A, **8** color B
- **14** 15º seed beads
- beading thread
- **2** 7 mm jump rings
- pair of marquise earring wires
- **2** pairs of chainnose pliers, or chainnose and roundnose pliers
- beading needle
- scissors

1 For each earring: Cut a 6-in. (15 cm) piece of beading thread. On the thread, center an alternating pattern of four color A bicone crystals and four 15ºs. Tie a surgeon's knot (Basics). String one end through the adjacent 15º.

2 On one end, string a color B bicone, a 15º, and a B. On the other end, string a B, a 15º, a B, and a 15º. Tie a surgeon's knot. String the ends back through the adjacent beads and trim the excess thread.

3 Open a jump ring (Basics). Attach the dangle and an earring wire. Close the jump ring.

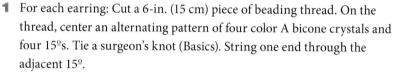

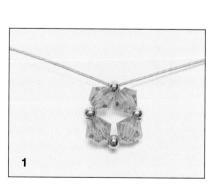

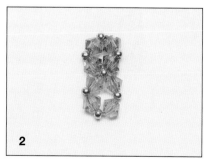

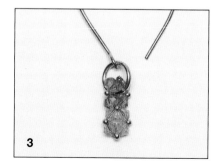

Two Steps to Style

designed by Irina Miech

SUPPLIES

- **2** 20 mm cones
- **2** 8 mm round crystals
- **2** 3 mm bicone crystals
- **2** 2-in. (5 cm) head pins
- pair of earring wires
- chainnose and roundnose pliers
- diagonal wire cutters

1 On a head pin, string a round crystal, a cone, and a bicone crystal. Make a wrapped loop (Basics).

2 Open the loop of an earring wire (Basics). Attach the dangle and close the loop. Make a second earring.

1

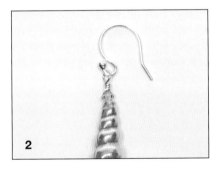

2

DESIGN OPTION

Try different cone and bead combinations for a virtually endless variety of looks.

✳ Tip

The size of the opening (not the size of the cone itself) will determine how large a bead you'll need.

Geometric Jewels

designed by Naomi Fujimoto

SUPPLIES

- **2** 25–30 mm marquise-shaped pendants or top-drilled beads
- **2** 35–40 mm marquise links
- 6 in. (15 cm) 24-gauge half-hard wire
- pair of earring wires
- chainnose and roundnose pliers
- diagonal wire cutters
- bench block or anvil
- hammer

1 On a bench block or anvil, hammer each side of a marquise link.

2 Cut a 3-in. (7.6 cm) piece of wire. String a pendant or top-drilled bead and make a set of wraps above it (Basics). Make the first half of a wrapped loop (Basics) perpendicular to the bead.

3 Attach the loop and the marquise link. Complete the wraps.

4 Open the loop of an earring wire (Basics). Attach the link and close the loop. Make a second earring.

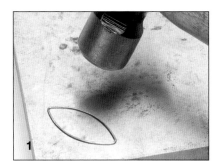

1

2

3

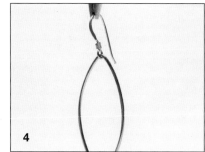

4

Wrapped Elegance

designed by Diane Whiting

SUPPLIES

- **2** 18 mm twist crystals
- **2** 14 mm twist crystals
- flexible beading wire, .015, in satin gold
- **2** crimp beads
- **2** crimp covers
- pair of lever-back earring wires
- crimping pliers
- diagonal wire cutters

1 Cut a 20-in. (51 cm) piece of beading wire. Center an 18 mm twist crystal on the wire. With one end, go around and through the crystal twice.

2 With the other end, go around and through the crystal once, then over the front of the crystal, anchoring the wire under a previous wrap.

3 Over both ends, string a 14 mm twist crystal. With both ends, go around and through the crystal twice.

4 Over both ends, string a crimp bead and the loop of an earring wire. Go back through the crimp bead and tighten the wire. Crimp the crimp bead (Basics) and trim the excess wire. Close a crimp cover over the crimp. Make a second earring.

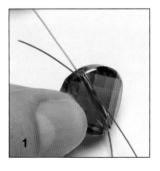

Flared Flowers

designed by Naomi Fujimoto

SUPPLIES

- **2** 31 mm Lucite trumpet flower beads
- **18** 4 mm bicone crystals
- 2½ in. (6.4 cm) cable chain, 2 mm links
- **18** 1½-in. (3.8 cm) 26-gauge head pins
- **2** 2-in. (5 cm) 24-gauge head pins
- pair of earring wires
- chainnose and roundnose pliers
- diagonal wire cutters

Trumpet flower beads from The Hole Bead Shoppe,
theholebeadshoppe.com.

1 For each earring: On a 1½-in. (3.8 cm) head pin, string a bicone crystal. Make the first half of a wrapped loop (Basics). Make nine bicone units.

2 On a 2-in. (5 cm) head pin, string a flower bead. Make the first half of a wrapped loop.

3 Cut a 1¼-in. (3.2 cm) piece of chain. Attach a bicone unit to the bottom link and complete the wraps. Attach a bicone unit to every other link, completing the wraps as you go.

4 Attach the bottom link and the loop of the flower unit. Complete the wraps.

5 Open the loop of an earring wire (Basics) and attach the dangle. Close the loop.

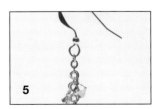

Gorgeous Blooms

designed by Naomi Fujimoto

SUPPLIES

- **2** 21 mm crystal briolettes
- **2** 16 mm metal lily pad blooms
- **2** 7 mm jump rings
- pair of earring wires
- chainnose and roundnose pliers, or **2** pairs of chainnose pliers

1 Open a jump ring (Basics). Attach a briolette and a loop of a lily pad bloom. Close the jump ring.

2 Open the loop of an earring wire (Basics). Attach the dangle and close the loop. Make a second earring.

DESIGN OPTIONS

Earrings aren't just a side note: Try different flower (or leaf) arrangements.

Dangling Flowers

designed by Sandy Parpart

SUPPLIES

- **2** 20–30 mm flower components
- **4** 6 mm crystals
- **4** 6 mm bugle or tube beads
- **2** 6 mm flat spacers
- 6 in. (15 cm) 22-gauge wire
- pair of earring posts with loop, plus ear nuts
- chainnose and roundnose pliers
- diagonal wire cutters

1 Cut a 3-in. (7.6 cm) piece of wire. Make the first half of a wrapped loop on one end (Basics). String: bugle or tube bead, crystal, spacer, crystal, and bugle or tube. Make the first half of a wrapped loop perpendicular to the previous loop.

2 Attach one loop to a flower component and complete the wraps. Attach the other loop to an earring post and complete the wraps. Make a second earring.

1

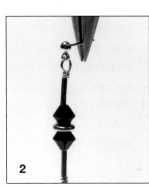

2

Amethyst Circles

designed by Jenny Van

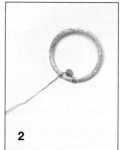

SUPPLIES

- **36** 3 mm round crystals
- **2** 20 mm hammered rings
- 40 in. (1 m) 28-gauge wire
- **2** 5 mm jump rings
- pair of earring posts and ear nuts
- **2** pairs of pliers
- diagonal wire cutters

1 Cut a 12-in. (30 cm) piece of wire. Secure the end by wrapping it tightly three times around a 20 mm ring.

2 String a crystal. Holding the bead inside the ring, wrap the wire twice around the ring. Repeat 11 times.

3 Cut an 8-in. (20 cm) piece of wire. Center the ring and wrap each end once around the ring.

4 On each end, string three crystals, curving them over the three crystals from steps 1 and 2. Wrap each end three times around the ring. Trim the excess wire and tuck the end.

5 Open a jump ring (Basics) and attach the beaded ring and the loop of an earring post. Close the jump ring. Make a second earring.

1

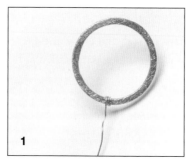

2

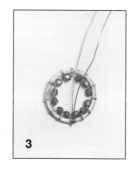

3

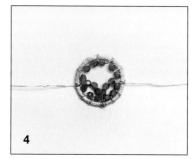

4

5

Opal Drops

designed by Naomi Fujimoto

SUPPLIES

- **2** 46 mm marquise-shaped tumbled glass pendants
- **10** 8–18 mm tumbled glass chips
- **2** 6 mm bicone crystals
- 8 in. (20 cm) 20-gauge wire
- chainnose and roundnose pliers
- diagonal wire cutters
- hammer and bench block
- metal file or emery board
- pen barrel

1 For each earring: Cut a 4-in. (10 cm) piece of wire. Using the largest part of your roundnose pliers, make the first half of a wrapped loop (Basics). Attach a pendant and complete the wraps.

2 String five chips and a bicone crystal. Make a right-angle bend parallel to the loop.

3 Curve the wire around a pen barrel. Trim the excess wire and curve the end upward. File the end.

4 On a bench block, gently hammer the curve of the wire.

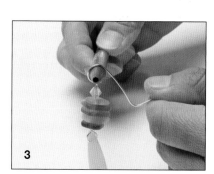

Winged Style

designed by Denise Yezbak Moore

SUPPLIES

- **2** 20 mm Venetian coin beads
- **2** 17 mm dragonfly charms
- **2** 10 mm round crystals
- **2** 10 mm bead caps
- ½ in. (1.3 cm) cable chain, 3 mm links
- **2** 2-in. (5 cm) head pins
- **2** 4 mm jump rings
- pair of earring wires
- chainnose and roundnose pliers
- diagonal wire cutters

1 Cut three links of chain. On a head pin, string a 10 mm round crystal, a bead cap, a Venetian bead, and an end link of the chain. Make a wrapped loop (Basics).

2 Open a 4 mm jump ring (Basics). Attach a dragonfly charm to the chain and close the jump ring. Open the loop of an earring wire (Basics) and attach the dangle. Close the loop. Make a second earring.

1

2

Beautiful Bounty

designed by Madelin Adriani Pratama

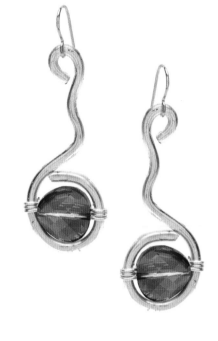

SUPPLIES

- **2** 12–22 mm beads
- 10-gauge Artistic Wire
- 10 in. (25 cm) 20-gauge Artistic Wire
- pair of earring wires
- chainnose and roundnose pliers
- diagonal wire cutters
- heavy-duty wire cutters
- hammer and bench block
- ring mandrel

1 Leave the 10-gauge wire on the roll and pull the end around a ring mandrel, making a loop large enough to accommodate a bead. Using heavy-duty wire cutters, trim the end. Trim the stem to about 2 in. (5 cm).

2 Use roundnose pliers to curve the stem as desired. Make a loop at the end of the stem. Hammer the front side of the wire.

3 Cut a 5-in. (13 cm) piece of 20-gauge wire. Center a bead on the wire. Positioning the bead inside the large loop, wrap each end of the 20-gauge wire around the 10-gauge wire three or four times. Trim the excess wrapping wire and tuck the ends.

4 Open the loop of an earring wire (Basics). Attach the dangle and close the loop. Make a second earring the mirror image of the first.

✺ Tip

To cut the 10-gauge wire, you can use memory-wire cutters in place of heavy-duty wire cutters.

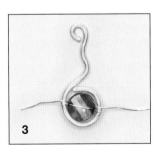

1

2

3

4

DESIGN OPTION

Make different shapes for all kinds of interesting combinations.

Triple-Loop Earrings

designed by Sonia Kumar

SUPPLIES

- **6** 8–10 mm round beads
- 12 in. (30 cm) 16-gauge dead-soft wire
- 18 in. (46 cm) 28-gauge half-hard wire
- pair of earring wires
- chainnose and roundnose pliers
- diagonal wire cutters
- cylindrical object, 8–10 mm diameter

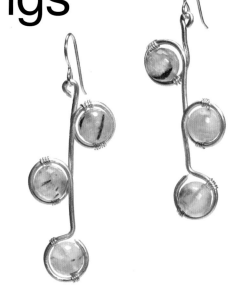

1 Cut a 6-in. (15 cm) piece of 16-gauge wire. Wrap one end around a cylindrical object to make a loop. Make a right-angle bend above the loop.

2 About ½ in. (1.3 cm) from the bend, form a second loop in the opposite direction. About ½ in. (1.3 cm) from the second loop, form a third loop in the same direction as the first.

3 About ½ in. (1.3 cm) from the third loop, use your roundnose pliers to form a small loop.

4 Cut a 3-in. (7.6 cm) piece of 28-gauge wire. Center a bead on the wire and place it in the bottom loop. Wrap each end around the loop. Repeat with the other loops.

5 Open the small loop and attach an earring wire. Close the loop. Repeat to make a second earring in the mirror image of the first.

DESIGN OPTION
Make super-easy earrings with one loop at the bottom. Hammer the wire for sturdiness.

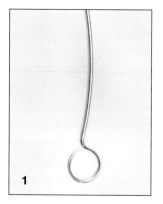

1

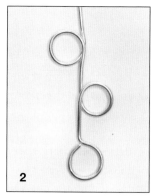

2

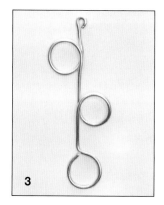

3

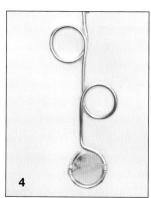

4

Perfect Posts

designed by Heather Boardman

SUPPLIES

- **2** 15 mm disk beads
- 8 in. (20 cm) 20-gauge half-hard wire
- pair of metal ear nuts
- chainnose and roundnose pliers
- diagonal wire cutters
- bench block or anvil
- emery board or file
- hammer

1 Cut a 4-in. (10 cm) piece of wire. Pull the ends of the wire together around the tip of your roundnose pliers to form an elongated U shape.

2 Bend the wire around your roundnose pliers to form three more U shapes.

3 Pinch the base of each U together with the tip of your roundnose pliers. Pull each U around to form a clover shape.

4 Bend each end to form a right angle. Hammer the clover on a bench block or anvil.

5 String a disk bead over both ends of the wire. With one end, make a coil around the other. Trim the excess wrapping wire.

6 Trim the remaining wire to ½ in. (1.3 cm) and file the end. Make a second earring.

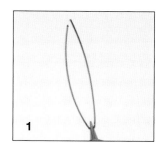

1

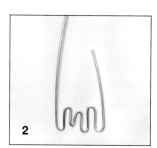

2

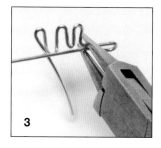

3

4

5

6

DESIGN OPTION

For dangles, harness disk beads with a simple wire wrap. Use 24- or 26-gauge wire to make organic wraps with your fingers.

❋ Tip

For more symmetrical wire shapes, form the wires for both earrings at the same time.

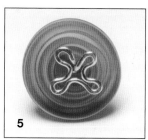

Dripping with Style

designed by Laurie-Ann Clinton

SUPPLIES

- **2** 29 mm circle pendants
- **12** 10 mm glass teardrop beads
- **12** 7 mm jump rings
- **2** 6 mm jump rings
- pair of hammered earring posts with loop, plus ear nuts
- chainnose and roundnose pliers, or **2** pairs of chainnose pliers

1 Open a 7 mm jump ring (Basics). Attach a teardrop bead to a circle pendant. Close the jump ring. Attach a total of six teardrops.

2 Use a 6 mm jump ring to attach the dangle and the loop of an earring post. Make a second earring.

DESIGN OPTION
Add single teardrops to the loops of chandelier components for a different look.

Pretty Palettes

designed by Kristina Henning

SUPPLIES

- **2** 17–20 mm briolettes
- **2** 5 mm pearls
- **32** 3–4 mm rondelles
- **10–14** 3 mm bicone crystals
- 6 in. (15 cm) 24-gauge wire
- **44–48** 1-in. (2.5 cm) 26- or 28-gauge decorative head pins
- pair of earring wires
- chainnose and roundnose pliers
- diagonal wire cutters

1 Make bead units: On a decorative head pin, string a 3–4 mm rondelle. Make the first half of a wrapped loop (Basics). Make 32 rondelle units, 10 to 14 bicone units, and two pearl units.

2 Make clusters: Attach the loops of five or six bead units. Complete the wraps as you go. For each earring, make a cluster of 13 units and two clusters of three units, leaving one loop unwrapped on each cluster.

3 For each earring: Cut a 3-in. (7.6 cm) piece of 24-gauge wire. String a briolette and make a set of wraps above it (Basics). Make a wrapped loop (Basics).

4 Attach two three-unit clusters, two bead units, and the loop of the briolette. Complete the wraps as you go.

5 Open the loop of an earring wire (Basics). Attach the loop of the briolette, the 13-unit cluster, and one to three bead units. Close the loop.

DESIGN OPTION

Using coiled fine-gauge wire and a few small beads, make a large, freeform wrap above a briolette.

Shades of the Shoreline

designed by Naomi Fujimoto

SUPPLIES

- **2** 11 mm Venetian glass square beads
- 10 in. (25 cm) 20-gauge wire
- 6 in. (15 cm) 26-gauge wire
- **2** pairs of pliers, including chainnose
- diagonal wire cutters
- hammer
- bench block or anvil
- pen barrel

1 For each earring: Cut a 5-in. (13 cm) piece of 20-gauge wire. Using chainnose pliers, make a right-angle bend about 2 in. (5 cm) from one end.

2 Continue making right-angle bends about ½ in. (1.3 cm) apart to form a square.

3 With the longer end, make a right-angle bend upward at the center of the side of the square. Wrap the shorter end around the longer wire. Trim the excess wrapping wire.

4 On a bench block or anvil, gently hammer each side of the square.

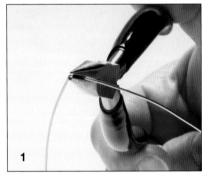

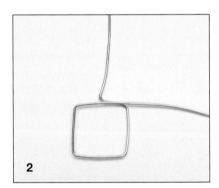

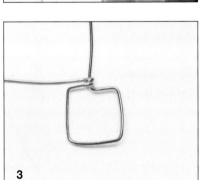

5 Cut a 3-in. (7.6 cm) piece of 26-gauge wire. Center a bead on the wire. Wrap each end of the 26-gauge wire around the wire frame four or five times. Trim the excess wrapping wire and tuck the end with chainnose pliers.

6 Make a 45-degree bend with the long wire. Pull the wire in the opposite direction around a pen barrel. Trim the excess wire if necessary and use chainnose pliers to curve the tip of the wire upward.

7 Hammer the curved part of the wire.

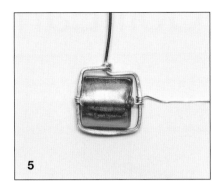

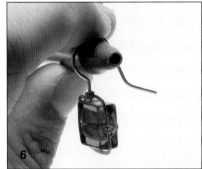

DESIGN OPTION

Pair cool colors like light aqua with silver wire. Hammer premade rectangular earring wires to give them some texture, then attach the beads with plain loops.

Disk-and-Coil Earrings

designed by Heather Boardman

SUPPLIES

BLUE-AND-PURPLE EARRINGS

- **2** 15–20 mm disk beads, center drilled
- 14 in. (36 cm) 20-gauge half-hard wire
- pair of earring wires

GREEN EARRINGS

- **2** 15–20 mm disk beads, center drilled
- 18 in. (46 cm) 20-gauge half-hard wire
- metal file or emery board
- Fiskars Right Angle mandrel (optional)

BOTH

- chainnose and roundnose pliers
- diagonal wire cutters
- round-barreled pen, knitting needle, or other cylindrical object

Disk beads from HMB Studios, hmbstudios.com.

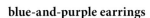

blue-and-purple earrings

1 Cut a 7-in. (18 cm) piece of wire. String a disk. About 1¼ in. (3.2 cm) from one end, bend the wire around the disk. Wrap the short wire around the longer wire and trim the excess.

2 Wrap the wire around a pen barrel or knitting needle three to five times. Use your fingers to adjust the coils.

3 Wrap the wire around the jaw of your roundnose pliers twice, making two loops parallel to the disk. Trim the excess wire.

4 Open the loop of an earring wire (Basics). Attach the dangle and close the loop. Make a second earring.

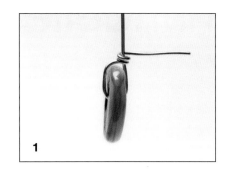

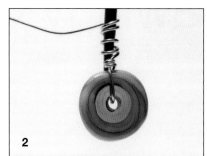

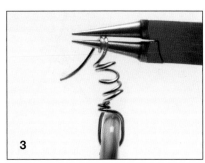

green earrings

1 Cut a 9-in. (23 cm) piece of wire. Follow steps 1 and 2 of the blue-and-purple earrings. Bend the wire upward at a right angle, centering it above the coils. Wrap the wire around a mandrel or other cylindrical object to make an earring wire. Trim the excess wire.

2 About ⅛ in. (3 mm) from the end, bend the wire upward with chainnose pliers. File the end. Make a second earring.

Swingy Chandeliers

designed by Karen Galbraith

SUPPLIES

- **2** 9 mm glass teardrops
- **12** 6 mm glass teardrops
- **12** 11º seed beads
- flexible beading wire, .014 or .015
- 8 in. (20 cm) 22-gauge wire
- **4** crimp beads
- **4** crimp covers
- pair of earring wires
- chainnose and roundnose pliers
- crimping pliers
- diagonal wire cutters

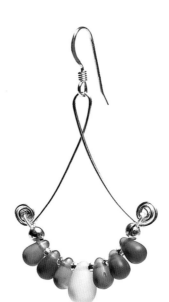

1. Cut a 3-in. (7.6 cm) piece of beading wire. Center a 9 mm teardrop. On each end, string an alternating pattern of three 11º seed beads and three 6 mm teardrops.
2. Cut a 4-in. (10 cm) piece of 22-gauge wire. Grasp the center of the wire with roundnose pliers and cross the ends of the wire to make a loop.
3. On one end of the wire, use the tip of your roundnose pliers to make a tiny loop. Use chainnose pliers to make a coil. Repeat on the other end.

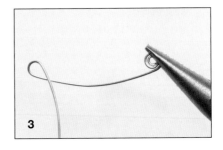

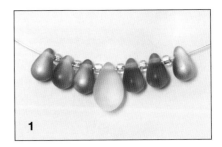

4 On each end of the beaded strand, string a crimp bead and the center of a coil. Go back through the last few beads strung and tighten the wire. Crimp the crimp bead (Basics) and trim the excess wire.

5 Use crimping pliers to gently close a crimp cover over each crimp.

6 Open the loop of an earring wire (Basics). Attach the dangle and close the loop. Make a second earring.

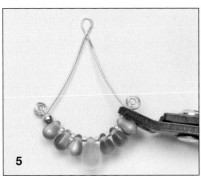

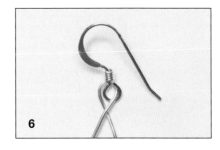

✳ Tip
Substitute fringe beads for the 6 mm teardrops.

Holiday Charm

designed by Liisa Turunen

SUPPLIES

- **18** 6 mm crystal channel charms

- 3½ in. (8.9 cm) chain, 5 mm links

- **4** 5–6 mm jump rings

- pair of earring wires

- **2** pairs of pliers (chainnose, roundnose, and/or bentnose)

- diagonal wire cutters

1 Open a jump ring (Basics) and attach three channel charms. Close the jump ring. Open a second jump ring and attach six charms. Close the jump ring.

2 Cut a 1½-in. (3.8 cm) piece of chain. Attach the six-charm jump ring to the end link. Attach the three-charm jump ring to the seventh link.

3 Open the loop of an earring wire (Basics) and attach the dangle. Make a second earring.

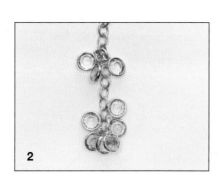

DESIGN OPTION

Dangle channel charms in a rainbow of colors from folded silver chain.

Soft Steampunk

designed by Lorelei Eurto

SUPPLIES

- **2** 19 mm gear beads, center drilled
- **2** 4 mm flat spacers
- **4** 3 mm round spacers
- 8 in. (20 cm) 20-gauge wire
- **2** crimp beads
- chainnose pliers
- diagonal wire cutters
- bench block or anvil
- file or emery board
- Fiskars Right Angle mandrel or thick pen
- hammer

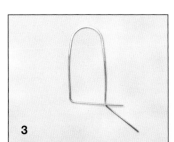

1 For both earrings: Cut a 4-in. (10 cm) piece of wire. Center the wire on the third tier of a Right Angle mandrel or the barrel of a thick pen. Pull the ends around to form an elongated U.

2 On a bench block or anvil, hammer the curve of the wire. Turn the wire over and hammer the other side.

3 About 1 in. (2.5 cm) from one end, bend the wire to form a 90-degree angle. About 1 in. (2.5 cm) from the other end, bend the wire to form a 45-degree angle.

4 String: round spacer, flat spacer, gear bead, round spacer, and crimp bead. Flatten the crimp bead (Basics).

5 Make a 90-degree bend next to the crimp. About ¼ in. (6 mm) from each end, trim the wire. File the ends.

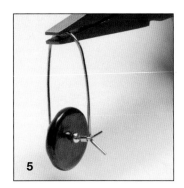

✳ Tip

Rather than making one earring at a time, try working with two 4-in. (10 cm) wires together. You'll get more consistent results that way.

A Night to Sparkle

designed by Jenny Van

1 Cut a 3½-in. (8.9 cm) piece of wire. On one end, make the first half of a wrapped loop (Basics). String a rondelle and make the first half of a wrapped loop. Make two 12 mm rondelle units.

2 On a head pin, string a round crystal and make the first half of a wrapped loop. Make 12 round-crystal dangles.

3 For each earring: Cut 12 ¼–1-in. (6 mm–2.5 cm) pieces of chain. Attach the chains to one loop of a 12 mm rondelle unit. On the other loop, attach a two-link chain. Complete the wraps.

4 Complete the wraps on two round crystal dangles. Open the loop of an earring wire (Basics). Attach a round crystal dangle, the top link of chain, and a round crystal dangle. Close the loop.

5 On each of the two top links, attach two round crystal dangles. Complete the wraps.

SUPPLIES

- **2** 12 mm crystal rondelles
- **12** 4 mm round crystals
- 6 in. (15 cm) 22-gauge half-hard wire
- 20–24 in. (51–61 cm) cable chain, 2 mm links
- **12** 1½-in. (3.8 cm) head pins
- pair of earring wires
- chainnose and roundnose pliers
- diagonal wire cutters

✳ Tip

When shopping for crystals online, look for a site that allows you to browse crystals by size or shape.

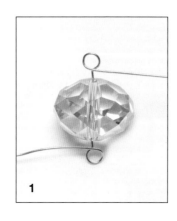

1

2–5

Bird Charms

designed by Jane Konkel

SUPPLIES

- **2** 5–10 mm beads
- **2** 4 mm peridot beads
- **2** 4 mm amethyst beads
- **2** 3 mm spacers
- 1 in. (2.5 cm) chain, 2–3 mm links
- **4** 1-in. (2.5 cm) head pins
- pair of earring wires
- chainnose and roundnose pliers
- diagonal wire cutters

1 For each earring: On a head pin, string a peridot bead and a spacer. Make a wrapped loop (Basics). Trim the head from a head pin and make a plain loop. String a 5–10 mm bead and an amethyst bead. Make a plain loop (Basics).

2 Cut a ½-in. (1.3 cm) piece of chain. Open the top loop (Basics) of the plain-loop unit and attach the end link. Close the loop. Open the bottom loop and attach the peridot unit. Close the loop.

3 Open the loop of an earring wire. Attach the dangle and close the loop.

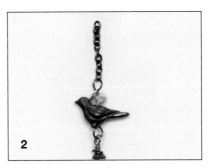

Hoop-De-Doo

designed by Ann Westby

SUPPLIES

- **2** 9–13 mm briolettes or teardrop-shaped beads, top drilled
- **2** 40–50 mm metal hoops
- 76 in. (1.9 m) 28-gauge wire
- pair of earring wires
- chainnose and roundnose pliers
- diagonal wire cutters

1 Cut a 16-in. (41 cm) piece of wire. Leaving a 2-in. (5 cm) tail, wrap the wire snugly around a hoop.

2 Continue wrapping the wire, covering about ¼ in. (6 mm) of the hoop.

3 Make a wrapped loop (Basics) but don't trim the excess wire.

4 Continue wrapping the wire around ¼ in. (6 mm) of the hoop. Trim the excess wire and tuck the ends with chainnose pliers.

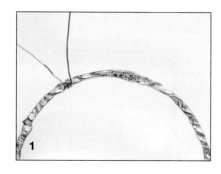

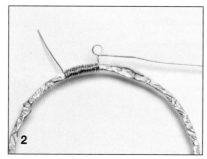

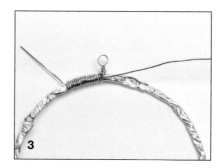

5 Repeat steps 1 to 4 on the opposite side of the hoop.

6 Cut a 6-in. (15 cm) piece of wire. String a briolette and make a set of wraps above it (Basics). Make the first half of a wrapped loop perpendicular to the briolette.

7 Attach the briolette unit to one of the loops of the hoop. Complete the wraps, covering part of the briolette if desired. Open the loop of an earring wire (Basics). Attach the hoop and close the loop. Make a second earring.

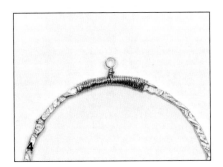

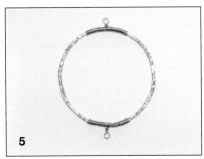

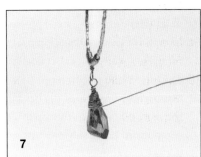

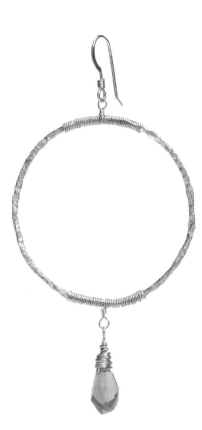

✳ Tips

• Choose delicate (and not overly large) briolettes that won't overwhelm the tiny wire wraps.

• For a more affordable pair of earrings, use craft wire instead of sterling or gold-filled.

• It's handy to have a 2-in. (5 cm) tail when you begin the wraps. The extra wire will allow you to make additional wraps if you need to even out the sides.

• If you use handmade hoops, you might find slight variations in size or shape.

Color Quest

designed by Jane Konkel

SUPPLIES

- **26** 6 mm rondelles, 10 in dominant color, 10 in second color, 6 in third color
- **14** 4 mm flat spacers
- **2** 50 mm crescent moon components
- **10** leaves from leaf chain, 5 mm links
- **3** in. (7.6 cm) flat-cable chain, 3 mm links
- **4** 4 mm jump rings
- pair of earring wires
- **12** 2-in. (5 cm) head pins or eye pins
- chainnose and roundnose pliers
- diagonal wire cutters

1 Trim the head from a head pin and make a plain loop (Basics) or use an eye pin. String: color B rondelle, spacer, color A rondelle, spacer, and color B rondelle. Make a plain loop.

2 Open a loop (Basics) of the bead unit and attach the second hole from the top of a crescent moon component. Close the loop. Attach the remaining loop to the hole on the other side.

3 Trim the head from a head pin and make a plain loop or use an eye pin. String a color A, a flat spacer, and a color C. Make a plain loop. On one end, attach a leaf unit. Make five bead units as shown.

4 Attach the top loop of the center dangle to the bottom hole of the crescent moon. Attach the remaining dangles on each side of the center dangle.

5 Cut a 1½-in. (3.8 cm) piece of flat cable chain, making sure to cut an odd number of links. Attach the center link and the loop of an earring wire.

6 Use a jump ring to attach each end of the chain and a top loop of the crescent. Make a second earring.

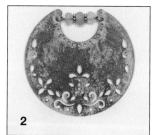

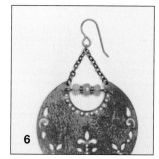

Layered Leaves

designed by Candie Cooper

SUPPLIES

- **20** 8–9 mm leaf charms in three finishes
- **2** 8 mm round crystals
- **2** 3–4 mm flat spacers
- 4 in. (10 cm) chain, 3–4 mm links
- **2** 1½-in. (3.8 cm) decorative head pins
- **24** 3–4 mm jump rings
- pair of earring wires
- chainnose and roundnose pliers
- diagonal wire cutters

1 On a decorative head pin, string a crystal and a spacer. Make a wrapped loop (Basics).

2 Cut a 10-link piece of chain. Open a jump ring (Basics) and attach the crystal unit and the bottom link. Close the jump ring. Use a jump ring to attach an earring wire and the top link.

3 Use jump rings to attach a leaf to each link. Make a second earring.

1

2

3

Fabulous Fans

designed by Jessica Tiemens

SUPPLIES

- **2** 6 mm crystal rondelles
- **14** 4 mm bicone crystals
- 38 in. (97 cm) chain, 1–2 mm links
- 9 in. (23 cm) 24-gauge half-hard wire
- **2** 4 mm jump rings
- pair of earring wires
- chainnose and roundnose pliers
- diagonal wire cutters

1 Cut a 2½-in. (6.4 cm) piece of wire. Make a wrapped loop (Basics). String a rondelle and make the first half of a wrapped loop perpendicular to the first loop.

2 Cut a 2-in. (5 cm) piece of wire. Make a small plain loop (Basics) on one end. Cut eight 2¼-in. (5.7 cm) pieces of chain. String a chain and a bicone crystal. String alternating chains and bicones, ending with a chain. Make a plain loop.

3 Attach the other ends of the chains to the unwrapped loop of the rondelle unit. Complete the wraps.

4 Open a jump ring (Basics) and attach the dangle and the loop of an earring wire. Close the jump ring. Make a second earring.

1

2

3

4

DESIGN OPTION

Use shorter chains with larger links, and substitute one large-jump ring for the rondelle unit.

❋ Tip

You can omit the jump ring in step 4. Instead, make the loops parallel on the rondelle unit, then attach the loop of an earring wire.

Go for Baroque

designed by Naomi Fujimoto

SUPPLIES

- **2** 10–12 mm pearls
- **2** 4 mm bicone crystals
- **2** bead caps
- **2** 1½-in. (3.8 cm) head pins
- pair of earring wires
- chainnose and roundnose pliers
- diagonal wire cutters

1 On a head pin, string a pearl, a bead cap, and a bicone crystal. Make a wrapped loop (Basics).

2 Open the loop of an earring wire (Basics). Attach the dangle and close the loop. Make a second earring.

DESIGN OPTION

For dramatic earrings, fold a large filigree in half and attach a pearl unit where the ends meet. Use an 8–10 mm jump ring to attach the earring wire.

Chunky Chains

designed by Naomi Fujimoto

SUPPLIES

- **2** 7–10 mm beads
- **2** 1½-in. (3.8 cm) head pins
- 5 in. (13 cm) chain, 12 mm links
- 4 in. (10 cm) chain, 5–6 mm links
- **2** 5–6 mm jump rings
- pair of earring wires
- chainnose and roundnose pliers
- diagonal wire cutters
- heavy-duty wire cutters (optional)

1 Cut a five-link piece of 12 mm (large) chain. Cut a 2-in. (5 cm) piece of 5–6 mm (small) chain. Open a jump ring (Basics). Attach an end link of each chain and the loop of an earring wire. Close the jump ring.

2 Weave the small chain through every other link of the large chain.

3 On a head pin, string a bead. Make the first half of a wrapped loop (Basics). Attach both end links and complete the wraps. Make a second earring.

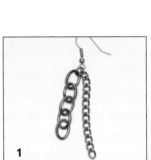

DESIGN OPTION

Use delicate chain to embellish seashells for earrings. To secure the wrapped chain, glue it to a few places in the back.

Twice as Nice

designed by Ute Bernsen

SUPPLIES

- **2** 9–25 mm charms
- **4** 5–6 mm crystals
- 2 in. (5 cm) chain, 3–4 mm links
- **4** 1½-in. (3.8 cm) head pins
- **2** 4–5 mm jump rings
- pair of earring wires
- chainnose and roundnose pliers
- diagonal wire cutters

1 On a head pin, string a crystal. Make a plain loop (Basics). Repeat.

2 Cut a ¾-in. (1.9 cm) piece of chain. Open a jump ring (Basics) and attach a charm and one end of the chain. Close the jump ring.

3 Open the loop of an earring wire (Basics) and attach the chain. Close the loop.

4 Open the loop of each crystal unit and attach the chain. Close the loop. Make a second earring.

1

2

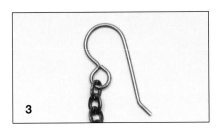

3

4

Mixed Metal Mania

designed by Mary Delaney

SUPPLIES

FILIGREE EARRINGS

- 24-gauge aluminum sheet
- **2** 15 mm filigree squares
- **2** 10 mm copper connectors
- **2** 5 mm jump rings
- pair of earring wires
- hole-punch pliers
- metal file
- shears
- texturing hammer (optional)

DISK EARRINGS

- **2** 4 mm beads
- 24-gauge metal sheet, in two styles
- 2 in. (5 cm) 22- or 24-gauge wire
- pair of earring wires
- chainnose and roundnose pliers
- diagonal wire cutters
- disk cutter
- hole-punch pliers
- metal file
- dowel (optional)

filigree earrings

1 Use shears to cut two triangles (about 30 mm) from a piece of aluminum sheet. If desired, use a hammer to texture the triangles. File the edges if necessary. Use hole-punch pliers to make a hole in each triangle.

2 For each earring: Open a jump ring (Basics). Attach the corner of a filigree, a triangle, and one hole of a copper connector. Close the jump ring.

3 Open the loop of an earring wire. Attach the dangle and close the loop.

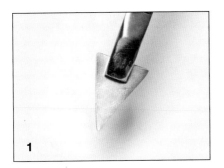

disk earrings

1 Insert a piece of metal sheet between the plates of a disk cutter. Place a punch in the coordinating hole in the plate.

2 Keeping the metal sheet stable, hammer the punch until it goes through the sheet. Remove the disk and punch (Tip). File the edges if necessary.

3 Use hole-punch pliers to make a hole in the disk. Make a total of four disks, two each in different styles.

4 For each earring: Cut a 1-in. (2.5 cm) piece of wire. Make a large plain loop (Basics) on one end. String a bead and make a plain loop perpendicular to the first.

5 Open the large loop of the bead unit. Attach the disks and close the loop. Open the top loop and attach an earring wire. Close the loop.

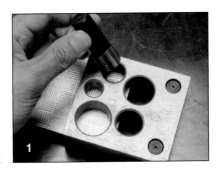

✺ Tips

• If a punch gets stuck in the plates of the disk cutter, turn the plates upside down. Place a dowel in the hole where the punch is and hammer the dowel until the punch dislodges.

• You can texture the metal sheet before or after you cut the shapes. If you texture the sheet before cutting, don't file too aggressively (you could damage the pattern).

Switching Style Gears

designed by Monica Han

SUPPLIES

- **2** 22 mm open-center gears
- **8** 6–7 mm jump rings
- pair of earring wires
- **2** pairs of pliers

1 Open a jump ring (Basics). Attach an open-center gear. Close the jump ring. Attach a second jump ring.

2 Use a pair of jump rings to attach the previous pair of jump rings and the loop of an earring wire. Make a second earring.

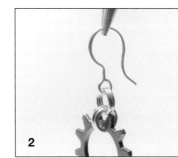

Quick Chain Mail

designed by Naomi Fujimoto

SUPPLIES

- **18** 11 mm enameled rings
- 4½ in. (11.4 cm) 20-gauge wire
- **64** 7 mm jump rings
- chainnose and roundnose pliers
- hammer and bench block
- metal file or emery board
- pen barrel

1

2

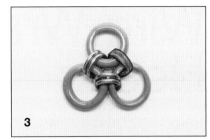

3

4

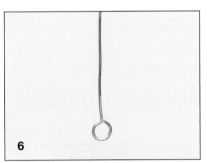

5

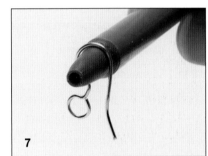

6

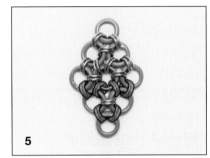

7

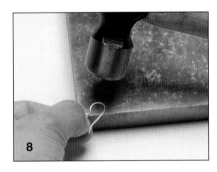

8

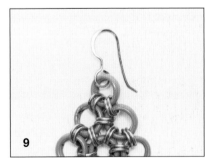

9

1 For each earring: Open a pair of jump rings (Basics). Attach two enameled rings and close the jump rings. Make a second two-ring segment.

2 To make a three-ring segment: Use two pairs of jump rings to attach three enameled rings.

3 Use two pairs of jump rings to attach an enameled ring to each enameled ring in a two-ring segment.

4 Use four pairs of jump rings to attach the three-ring segment and the new segment from step 3.

5 Use four pairs of jump rings to attach the three-ring segment and the second two-ring segment. Use two pairs of jump rings to attach the second two-ring segment and an enameled ring.

6 To make each earring wire: Cut a 2¼-in. (5.7 cm) piece of wire. Using the largest part of your roundnose pliers, make a plain loop (Basics) on one end.

7 Make a right-angle bend next to the loop. Wrap the wire around a pen barrel. Use chainnose pliers to make an upward bend near the end of the wire. Trim the excess wire and file the end.

8 On a bench block, gently hammer the curve of the earring wire. Turn over the earring wire and hammer the other side.

9 Open the loop of the earring wire. Attach the dangle and close the loop.

DESIGN OPTION
Use two or more hues to create color-blocked earrings.

Wire-Wrapped Hoops

designed by Felicia Cantillo

SUPPLIES

- **4** 9–10 mm faceted oval beads
- **38–42** 3 mm faceted round beads
- **20** 3 mm round spacers
- **20** 3 mm flat spacers
- 9 in. (23 cm) 18-gauge wire
- 80 in. (2 m) 26-gauge wire
- 3 in. (7.6 cm) chain, 3–4 mm links
- **12** 1½-in. (3.8 cm) head pins
- pair of earring wires
- chainnose and roundnose pliers
- nylon-jaw pliers (optional)
- diagonal wire cutters
- 1-in. (2.5 cm) diameter cylindrical object

1 On a head pin, string: round spacer, flat spacer, round bead, flat spacer, and round spacer. Make a wrapped loop (Basics). Make a second round bead unit. On a head pin, string: round spacer, flat spacer, oval bead, flat spacer, and round spacer. Make a wrapped loop. Set these bead units aside for step 5.

2 Make a round bead unit and an oval bead unit as in step 1, but do not complete the wraps. Cut a four-link and a five-link piece of chain. Attach the round bead unit to the four-link chain and complete the wraps. Attach the oval bead unit to the five-link chain and complete the wraps. Set the dangles aside for step 7.

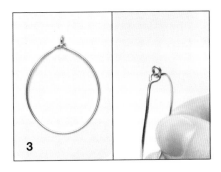

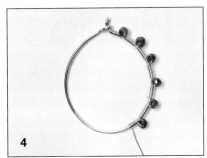

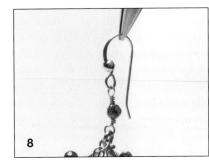

3 To make the earring frame: Cut a 4½-in. (11.4 cm) piece of 18-gauge wire. Wrap the wire around a cylindrical object so the ends cross. On each end, make a plain loop (Basics). Bend one loop so it is perpendicular to the other. Open the other loop (Basics), attach the wire to the stem, and close the loop.

4 Cut a 40-in. (1 m) piece of 26-gauge wire. At the top of the frame near a loop, wrap one end of the wire eight to 10 times. String a round bead, and make eight to 10 more wraps. Continue making wraps and stringing beads until just above the bottom of the frame. Make two to five wraps.

5 String a round-bead unit from step 1 and make five to eight wraps. String the oval-bead unit from step 1 and make five to eight wraps. String the remaining round bead unit and make two to five wraps.

6 Continue making wraps and stringing beads as in step 4 until you reach the other loop of the frame. Trim the excess wire and tuck the end.

7 Open the frame's perpendicular loop and attach the dangles from step 2. Close the loop.

8 Trim the head from a head pin and make the first half of a wrapped loop. String a round bead and make the first half of a wrapped loop. Attach one loop to the frame and the other loop to an earring wire and complete the wraps. Make a second earring the mirror image of the first.

✳ Tip

If 40 in. (1 m) of 26-gauge wire is too much for you to handle when wrapping, cut the wire in half and wrap with one 20-in. (51 cm) piece. When the wire gets short, end it as in step 6. Begin wrapping the next 20-in. piece where you left off.

Ball Chain Hoops

designed by Sonia Kumar

SUPPLIES

- **2** 6 mm round beads
- 5–6 in. (13–15 cm) ball chain
- memory wire, ring diameter
- 12 in. (30 cm) 24-gauge wire
- **2** 1½-in. (3.8 cm) head pins
- **2** 7 mm jump rings
- pair of earring wires
- chainnose and roundnose pliers
- diagonal wire cutters
- heavy-duty wire cutters

1 Use heavy-duty wire cutters to cut one complete ring from a memory wire coil. If you don't have heavy-duty wire cutters, grip the wire with chainnose pliers and bend it back and forth until it breaks. Never use jewelry-weight cutters on memory wire.

2 Wrap a piece of ball chain around the outside of the memory wire and trim to fit.

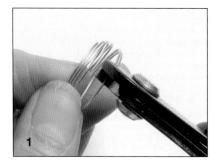

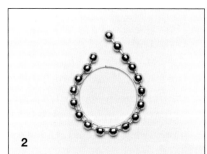

3 Cut a 6-in. (15 cm) piece of 24-gauge wire and wrap one end around the memory wire two or three times across from the break in the memory wire.

4 Wrap the 24-gauge wire around the chain between the first two balls and around the memory wire.

5 Continue wrapping the 24-gauge wire between the balls and around the memory wire until you reach the end of the chain.

6 Wrap the 24-gauge wire once around the memory wire and trim the excess wire.

7 On a head pin, string a bead and make a plain loop (Basics).

8 Open a jump ring (Basics). Attach the loop of an earring wire, the hoop, and the bead unit. Close the jump ring. Make a second earring.

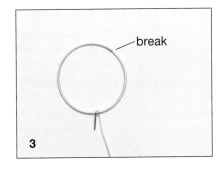

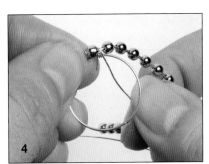

Wire Capture

designed by Allyson Giesen

SUPPLIES

- **2** 10–20 mm cabochons or undrilled stones
- 32 in. (81 cm) 20- or 22-gauge wire
- pair of earring wires
- chainnose and roundnose pliers
- diagonal wire cutters
- mandrel

1 For each earring: Cut a 16-in. (41 cm) piece of wire. Place your roundnose pliers at the center of the wire. Pull the ends around the pliers, making a loop to cradle the back of a cabochon.

2 Wrap the wire around the back and sides of the cabochon about six to eight times, making sure a few wraps overlap the front of the cabochon. Form the desired shape with the wire (Tip).

3 On one end, make a loop parallel with the cabochon. On the other end, make a small loop perpendicular to the first loop. Open the small loop (Basics) and attach the wire just below the parallel loop. Close the loop.

4 Open the loop of an earring wire. Attach the dangle and close the loop.

1

2

3

4

✿ Tip

If you don't have a mandrel to shape your wire, use another cylindrical object instead. A pill bottle works well.

Aquamarine Dangles

designed by Jane Konkel

SUPPLIES

- **2** 6 mm aquamarine rondelles
- 6 in. (15 cm) 24-gauge wire
- 6½ in. (16.5 cm) chain, 2–3 mm links
- **2** 3 mm jump rings (optional)
- pair of earring wires
- chainnose and roundnose pliers
- diagonal wire cutters

1   For each earring: Cut two 1½-in. (3.8 cm) pieces of chain. Cut a 3-in. (7.6 cm) piece of wire and make the first half of a wrapped loop (Basics). Attach an end link of one chain and complete the wraps. On the wire, string a rondelle and make the first half of a wrapped loop. Attach an end link of the other chain and complete the wraps.

2   Open a jump ring or a link of chain (Basics). Attach the end links of each chain and close the jump ring or chain link.

3   Open the loop of an earring wire and attach the dangle. Close the loop.

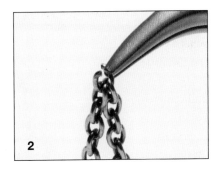

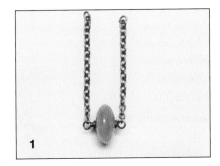

Cross Earrings

designed by Ann Westby

SUPPLIES

- **2** 20–25 mm cross or other flat beads
- 14 in. (36 cm) 20- or 22-gauge half-hard wire
- pair of earring wires
- chainnose and roundnose pliers
- diagonal wire cutters
- bench block or anvil
- hammer

For turquoise cross beads, visit Auntie's Beads, auntiesbeads.com, or Ny6Designs inc., ny6design.com.

1 Cut a 5-in. (13 cm) piece of wire. On one end, use the tip of your roundnose pliers to make a tiny loop.

2 Grasp the loop with chainnose pliers and continue coiling the wire with your fingers. Make the coil about ³⁄₈ in. (1 cm) in diameter. (Place it against a cross bead to determine the finished size.)

3 Make a right-angle bend centered above the coil. About ¼ in. (6 mm) from the bend, make a small wrapped loop (Basics).

4 Grasp the wrapped loop with chainnose pliers and bend it at a right angle to the coil. Gently hammer both sides of the coil. If the coil loosens after hammering, adjust it with your fingers.

5 Cut a 2-in. (5 cm) piece of wire. Make a tiny loop on one end. String a cross bead and the coil. Make a wrapped loop.

6 Open the loop of an earring wire (Basics). Attach the dangle and close the loop. Make a second earring the mirror image of the first.

DESIGN OPTION

For bold earrings, wrap 20-gauge wire around the triangular end of a Fiskars Right Angle mandrel.

Peridot Circles

designed by Cathy Jakicic

SUPPLIES

- **24** 7 mm oval peridot beads
- **2** 4 mm cube beads
- 14 in. (36 cm) half-hard 26-gauge wire
- pair of earring wires
- chainnose and roundnose pliers
- diagonal wire cutters

1 Cut a 7-in. (18 cm) piece of 26-gauge wire. String seven peridot beads, a cube bead, and five peridot beads. Wrap one wire around the other. Trim the excess wrapping wire.

2 Make a wrapped loop (Basics). Open the loop of an earring wire (Basics) and attach the dangle. Close the loop. Make a second earring. Use your fingers to shape the beaded loops as desired.

Coil, Then Stack

designed by Felicia Cantillo

SUPPLIES

- **2** 20–22 mm lentil beads
- **2** 7–8 mm faceted rondelles
- **32** 4–5 mm accent beads in two or three colors
- **4** 3–4 mm flat spacers
- 10 in. (25 cm) 20-gauge wire
- 4 ft. (1.2 m) 26-gauge wire
- **2** 7–9 mm cones
- pair of earring wires
- chainnose and roundnose pliers
- diagonal wire cutters

1 Cut a 1½-in. (3.8 cm) piece of 26-gauge wire. On one end, use the tip of your roundnose pliers to make a tiny loop. String an accent bead and make a wrapped loop (Basics). Make 16 bead units.

2 Cut a 5-in. (13 cm) piece of 20-gauge wire. On one end, use the tip of your roundnose pliers to make a tiny loop as in step 1.

3 Grasp the loop with chainnose pliers and continue coiling the wire with your fingers. Make the coil about ⁵⁄₁₆ in. (8 mm) in diameter.

4 String a lentil bead and bend the coil to the front of it. String: spacer, bead units, spacer, rondelle, and cone. Make a plain loop (Basics).

5 Open the loop of an earring wire (Basics) and attach the dangle. Close the loop. Make a second earring.

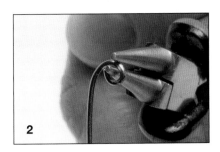

New Angle on Dangles

designed by Carolina Angel

SUPPLIES

- **2** 10–20 mm gemstone briolettes
- stardust beads
    - **2** 7 mm rounds
    - **8** 4 mm rondelles
    - **6** 4 mm rounds
    - **6** 3 mm rondelles
    - **2** 3 mm rounds
- **2** 3 mm bicone crystals
- flexible beading wire, .010
- **2** crimp beads
- pair of earring wires
- chainnose or crimping pliers
- diagonal wire cutters

1 Cut a 9-in. (23 cm) piece of beading wire and center a briolette. On each end, string a 3 mm rondelle, a 4 mm round, and a 4 mm rondelle.

2 Over both ends, string a 7 mm round, a 4 mm round, a 3 mm rondelle, and two 4 mm rondelles.

3 Over both ends, string a crimp bead, a 3 mm round, a bicone crystal, and the loop of an earring wire. Go back through the last few beads strung and tighten the wires. Crimp the crimp bead (Basics) and trim the excess wire. Make a second earring.

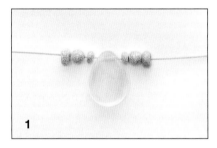

DESIGN OPTION

No beading wire? No problem! Make this pair of earrings with white nylon thread. Simply tie a knot (Basics) instead of using a crimp bead.

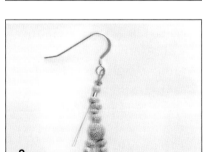

Study in Contrasts

designed by Naomi Fujimoto

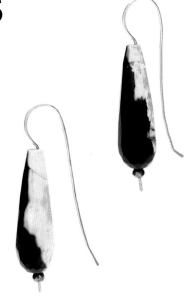

SUPPLIES

- **2** 30 mm faceted teardrop beads
- **2** 3 mm faceted rondelles
- 8 in. (20 cm) 20-gauge wire
- diagonal wire cutters
- hammer and bench block
- metal file or emery board
- pen

  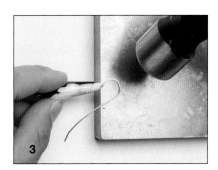

1 Set aside two rondelles that will accommodate 20-gauge wire. For each earring: Cut a 4-in. (10 cm) piece of wire. Hammer the end of the wire to form a paddle shape.

2 String a rondelle and a teardrop bead. Make a right-angle bend, then wrap the wire around a pen barrel. Trim the wire to about the length of the teardrop. File the end.

3 On a bench block, gently hammer each side of the wire.

DESIGN OPTION

Turn top-drilled pink amethyst beads into earrings by extending the wire wraps around each bead.

Style in Scale

designed by Christianne Camera

SUPPLIES

- **2** 12 mm coin beads
- **2** 26 mm rings
- **2** 2-in. (5 cm) head pins
- **2** 5–7 mm jump rings
- pair of earring wires
- chainnose and roundnose pliers
- diagonal wire cutters

1 For each earring: On a head pin, string a bead. Make the first half of a large wrapped loop (Basics).

2 Attach the bead unit and a ring. Complete the wraps.

3 Open a jump ring (Basics). Attach the wrapped loop and the loop of an earring wire. Close the jump ring.

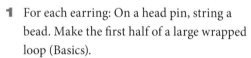

Inspired by Opposites

designed by Meredith Jensen

SUPPLIES

- **10** 7 mm heishi beads or rondelles
- **6** 6 mm round beads
- **6** 4 mm flat spacers
- **10** 4 mm bead caps
- **2** soldered jump rings
- 8 in. (20 cm) 24-gauge wire
- **6** 2-in. (5 cm) head pins
- pair of earring wires
- chainnose and roundnose pliers
- diagonal wire cutters

1 For each earring: On a head pin, string a round bead and a bead cap. Make a wrapped loop (Basics). Make three bead units.

2 Cut a 4-in. (10 cm) piece of wire. Make the first half of a wrapped loop. Attach each bead unit and complete the wraps.

3 String three spacers, a bead cap, five heishi beads, and a bead cap. Make the first half of a wrapped loop. Attach a soldered jump ring and complete the wraps, overlapping the excess wire.

4 Open the loop of an earring wire (Basics) and attach the dangle. Close the loop.

Prefab & Pretty

designed by Naomi Fujimoto

SUPPLIES

- 30–38 in. (76–97 cm) gemstone chain, 4 mm rondelles
- **2** cones
- 8 in. (20 cm) 24-gauge wire
- pair of earring wires
- chainnose and roundnose pliers
- diagonal wire cutters

1 For each earring: Cut three or four 14–link pieces of gemstone chain. Set aside one of the rondelles from a cut link.

2 Cut a 4-in. (10 cm) piece of wire. Make the first half of a wrapped loop (Basics) on one end. Attach this loop and the two center loops of each chain. Complete the wraps.

3 String a cone and the rondelle from step 1, and make a wrapped loop.

4 Open the loop of an earring wire (Basics). Attach the dangle and close the loop.

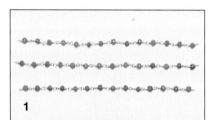

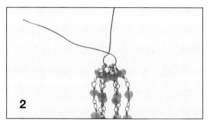

In the Chips

designed by Cathy Jakicic

SUPPLIES

- **6** 8–12 mm gemstone chips
- **2** 11º seed beads
- **2** 1½-in. (3.8 cm) head pins
- **2** 7 mm jump rings
- **2** loop halves of toggle clasps
- pair of earring wires
- chainnose and roundnose pliers
- diagonal wire cutters

1. On a head pin, string an 11º seed bead and three chips. Make the first half of a wrapped loop (Basics) using the largest part of your roundnose pliers. Attach the unit to a clasp half and complete the wraps.
2. Open a jump ring (Basics) and attach the dangle and an earring wire. Close the jump ring. Make a second earring.

Beader's Choice

designed by Cathy Jakicic

SUPPLIES

- **2** 16 mm teardrop beads, top drilled
- **4** 4 mm round Czech fire-polished crystals
- 6 in. (15 cm) 24-gauge half-hard wire
- pair of earring wires
- chainnose and roundnose pliers
- diagonal wire cutters

1. For each earring: Cut a 3-in. (7.6 cm) piece of wire. String a crystal, a teardrop bead, and a crystal. Make a set of wraps above the beads (Basics).
2. Make a wrapped loop (Basics). Open the loop of an earring wire (Basics) and attach the dangle. Close the loop.

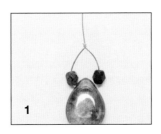
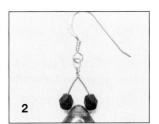

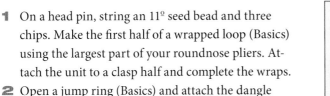

Celtic Pride

designed by Kelsey Lawler

SUPPLIES

- **2** 30 mm stick beads, center drilled
- **2** 14 mm round beads
- **4** 4 mm round crystals
- **2** 1½-in. (3.8 cm) head pins
- **2** 2-in. (5 cm) eye pins
- pair of earring wires
- chainnose and roundnose pliers
- diagonal wire cutters

1 For each earring: On a head pin, string a 14 mm bead. Make a plain loop (Basics).

2 On an eye pin, string a crystal, a stick bead, and a crystal. Make a wrapped loop (Basics).

3 Open the loop of the head pin unit (Basics). Attach the loop and the eye pin unit. Close the loop.

4 Open the loop of an earring wire. Attach the dangle and close the loop.

Crossed Wires

designed by Ann Westby

SUPPLIES

- **2** 15–20 mm nuggets
- **2** 10–13 mm briolettes
- 16 in. (41 cm) 24-gauge half-hard wire
- pair of earring wires
- chainnose and roundnose pliers
- diagonal wire cutters

1 Cut a 3-in. (7.6 cm) piece of wire. String a briolette and make a set of wraps above the bead (Basics).

2 Make the first half of a wrapped loop (Basics).

3 Cut a 5-in. (7.6 cm) piece of wire. Make a wrapped loop. String a nugget and make a wrapped loop. Do not trim the wire.

4 Bring the wire tail across the front of the nugget and around the bottom loop. Create an X with the wire and wrap it around the stem of the top loop. Trim the excess wire.

5 Attach the briolette unit to the nugget's bottom loop and complete the wraps.

6 Open the loop of an earring wire (Basics). Attach the wire and close the loop. Make a second earring.

1

2

3

4

5

6

Ruby Dangles

designed by Jenny Van

SUPPLIES

- **14** 4 mm round crystals
- **10** 3 mm bicone crystals
- **2** 4 mm spacers
- **2** 16 mm hammered rings
- **2** 12 mm hammered rings
- 8 in. (20 cm) 24-gauge half-hard wire
- 1 in. (2.5 cm) chain, 2 mm links
- **22** 1-in. (2.5 cm) head pins
- pair of earring wires
- chainnose and roundnose pliers
- diagonal wire cutters

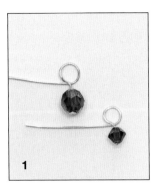 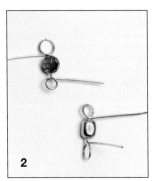 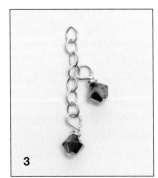

1 On a head pin, string a round crystal. Make the first half of a wrapped loop (Basics). Repeat, substituting a bicone crystal for the round. Make six round units and five bicone units.

2 Cut a 2-in. (5 cm) piece of wire. Make the first half of a wrapped loop on one end. String a round crystal and make the first half of a wrapped loop. Repeat, substituting a spacer for the round crystal and making the loop perpendicular to the first loop.

3 Cut a ½-in. (1.3 cm) piece of chain. Attach the loop of a bicone unit to one end. Skip two links and attach another bicone unit. Complete the wraps.

4 On one loop of the round unit from step 2, attach a round unit from step 1, the chain, and a round unit, completing the wraps as you go. Complete the wraps on the bottom loop of the round unit.

5 Attach a 16 mm ring to the top loop. Complete the wraps.

6 On each side of the chain dangle, attach a round unit, a bicone unit, and a round unit, completing the wraps as you go.

7 On one loop of the spacer unit, attach the 16 mm ring, a bicone unit, and a 12 mm ring. Complete the wraps.

8 Complete the wraps on the top loop. Open the loop of an earring wire (Basics) and attach the dangle. Close the loop. Make a second earring.

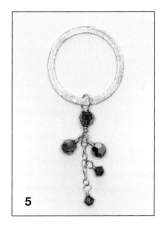

Pearl Drops

designed by Jenny Van

SUPPLIES

- **2** 12 mm coin pearls
- **4** 23 mm chandelier components, with four loops
- **2** 1½-in. (3.8 cm) head pins
- **6** 3–4 mm jump rings
- pair of decorative earring wires
- chainnose and roundnose pliers
- diagonal wire cutters

Chandelier components from Auntie's Beads, auntiesbeads.com.

1 On a head pin, string a coin pearl. Make the first half of a wrapped loop (Basics). Attach the single loop of a chandelier component as shown and complete the wraps. Open a jump ring (Basics) and attach an outer loop of a chandelier component and the corresponding loop of another component. Close the jump ring. Use jump rings to attach the remaining loops.

2 Open the loop of an earring wire (Basics). Attach the dangle and close the loop. Make a second earring to match the first.

Pearl Wonders

designed by Irina Miech

SUPPLIES

- **2** 8–12 mm pearls
- **16** 6 mm pearls, diagonally drilled
- 8 in. (20 cm) 24-gauge half-hard wire
- **2** 1½-in. (3.8 cm) head pins
- pair of earring wires
- chainnose and roundnose pliers
- diagonal wire cutters

1 On a head pin, string an 8–12 mm pearl and make a wrapped loop (Basics). Cut a 4-in. (10 cm) piece of wire. Make the first half of a wrapped loop (Basics) on one end. Attach the pearl unit and complete the wraps.

2 String eight 6 mm pearls and make a wrapped loop.

3 Open the loop of an earring wire (Basics). Attach the dangle and close the loop. Make a second earring.

❈ Tip

When wrapping the head pin around the 6 mm round pearl, pull the wire snugly against the pearl. Use thinner head pins for easier wrapping.

Swingy Sew-Ons

designed by Glenda Paunonen

SUPPLIES

- **2** 6 mm round pearls
- **80** 3 mm rice pearls
- 1 g 15º seed beads
- 2 yd. (1.8 m) thread
- **2** 14 mm mesh screens with backs
- flexible beading needle
- **2** 2-in. (5 cm) decorative head pins
- pair of earring wires
- chainnose and roundnose pliers
- diagonal wire cutters

1 For each earring: Cut a 1-yd. (.9 m) piece of thread and center a needle. From back to front, string the center hole of a mesh screen. String a 3 mm pearl and a 15º seed bead. (I've used red thread for steps 1 to 4 for illustrative purposes.)

2 Go back through the pearl and the center hole in the screen. Tighten the thread, leaving a 4-in. (10 cm) tail.

3 Tie a surgeon's knot (Basics).

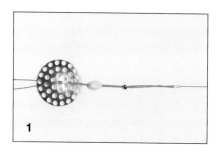

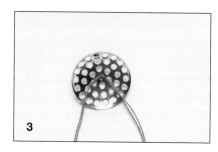

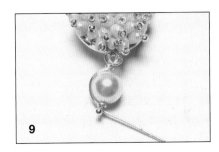

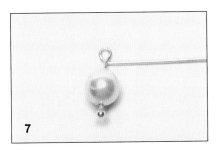

4 Working outward, continue to string one pearl and one 15º through each of the holes in the screen until you've strung all of the holes. Tie the threads on the back side of the screen after you've strung each set.

5 On the back of the screen, tie the ends of the thread together with several knots. Trim the excess thread.

6 Place the beaded screen in its back. Use chainnose pliers to carefully fold the prongs to hold the screen in place.

7 On a head pin, string a 6 mm pearl. Leaving about 1–2 mm on each side of the pearl, make the first half of a wrapped loop (Basics).

8 Attach the loop of the head pin unit and a loop of the back. Wrap the wire around the stem one and a half times above the pearl.

9 Bring the wire down around the pearl and wrap the wire once around the stem below the pearl.

10 Bring the wire back up around the pearl and complete the wraps above the pearl. Trim the excess wire.

11 Open the loop of an earring wire (Basics). Attach the dangle and close the loop.

Stylish Through & Through

designed by Dee Perry

SUPPLIES

- **2** 12 mm polygon crystals
- **8** 5 mm potato pearls
- 5 in. (13 cm) 22-gauge wire
- **8** 1½-in. (3.8 cm) head pins
- pair of earring wires
- chainnose and roundnose pliers
- diagonal wire cutters

1 Cut a 2½-in. (6.4 cm) piece of wire. Make a wrapped loop (Basics). String a polygon crystal and make a wrapped loop.

2 On a head pin, string a potato pearl. Make the first half of a wrapped loop. Make four pearl units.

3 Attach the pearl units to one loop of the polygon unit and complete the wraps. Open the loop of an earring wire (Basics). Attach the dangle and close the loop. Make a second earring.

Ombre Impression

designed by Kelsey Lawler

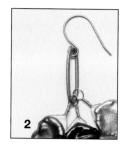

SUPPLIES

- **6** 12–16 mm keshi pearls, top drilled, in three colors
- 18 in. (46 cm) 24- or 26-gauge wire
- **2** 18 mm links of chain
- pair of earring wires
- chainnose and roundnose pliers
- diagonal wire cutters

1 For each earring: Make three pearl units by wrapping above 12 mm keshi pearl with 3-in. (7.6 cm) pieces of wire. Attach a link of chain and complete the wraps (Basics).

2 Open the loop of an earring wire (Basics). Attach the dangle and close the loop.

Stacked Pearls

designed by Miriam Fuld

SUPPLIES

- **2** 10 mm glass or crystal pearls
- **4** 8 mm glass or crystal pearls
- **4** 2 mm round spacers
- **2** 1½-in. (3.8 cm) head pins
- pair of kidney-style earring wires
- chainnose and roundnose pliers
- diagonal wire cutters

1 On a head pin, string: 10 mm pearl, 8 mm pearl, spacer, 8 mm, and spacer. Make a plain loop (Basics).

2 Slide the loop of the dangle onto a kidney-style earring wire. Use chainnose pliers to pinch the loop of the earring wire closed. Make a second earring.

Pearl
Starburst

designed by Glenda Paunonen

SUPPLIES

- **14–20** 4 mm round pearls
- **14–20** 3 mm drilled sequins or bicone crystals
- 22 in. (56 cm) 24-gauge wire
- **14–20** 1½–2-in. (3.8–5 cm) head pins
- **2** 5 mm jump rings
- pair of earring wires
- chainnose and roundnose pliers
- diagonal wire cutters

The 3 mm "sequins" are Swarovski Elements flatback crystals, article number 3112.

1 For each earring: Cut a 9–11-in. (23–28 cm) piece of wire. On a head pin, string a crystal and a pearl. String seven to 10 head pins. Gather the head pins in a bundle.

2 About ¾–1 in. (1.9–2.5 cm) from the bottom of the head pins, wrap the wire tightly around the bundle until there's ¼ in. (6 mm) of wire visible above the wraps. Trim the bottom end of the wrapping wire and tuck it close to the wraps.

3 On the end of each head pin, use your roundnose pliers to make a loop, turning the wire outward.

4 Trim the end of the wrapping wire to ½ in. (1.3 cm). Coil the wire around the tip of your roundnose pliers two or three times to make a coiled loop.

5 Open a jump ring (Basics). Attach the coiled loop and the loop of an earring wire. Close the jump ring.

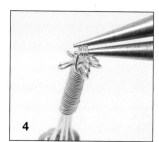

1

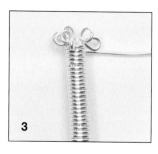

2

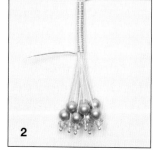

3

4

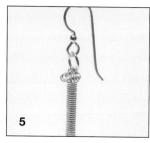

5

Luminous Blooms

designed by Ashley Bunting

SUPPLIES

- **2** 18 mm Lucite flowers
- **2** 14 mm Lucite flowers
- **2** 8 mm round crystals
- **4** 4 mm filigree spacers
- 2 in. (5 cm) chain, 5 mm links
- **4** 1½-in. (3.8 cm) head pins
- pair of earring wires
- chainnose and roundnose pliers
- diagonal wire cutters

1 For each earring: On a head pin, string a spacer and a crystal. Make the first half of a wrapped loop (Basics).

2 Cut a five-link piece of chain. Attach the bead unit and an end link. Complete the wraps.

3 On a head pin, string: spacer, 14 mm Lucite flower, 18 mm Lucite flower, and center chain link. With roundnose pliers, grasp the end of the head pin and roll the wire around to form a loop.

4 Open the loop of an earring wire (Basics). Attach the dangle and close the loop.

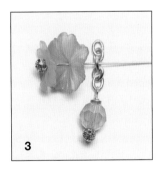

Four Easy Earrings

designed by Leslie Rogalski

SUPPLIES

TINY BUNCHES

- **2** 10 mm wood saucer beads, green
- **4** 6 mm wood round beads, vivid purple
- **8** 6º seed beads, metallic gold
- 6 in. (15 cm) 24-gauge wire
- 6 in. (15 cm) long-and-short chain, 9 mm and 5 mm links
- **2** 8 mm jump rings

STACKS

- **10** 6 mm wood round beads, vivid purple
- **12** 6º seed beads, metallic gold
- **2** 3-in. (7.6 cm) decorative head pins

DOUBLE DANGLES

- **4** 8 mm wood barrels, vivid purple
- **4** 6º seed beads, metallic copper
- 3 in. (7.6 cm) cable chain, 4 mm links
- 8 in. (20 cm) 24-gauge wire

WIRE SWIRLS

- **2** 6 mm wood round beads, vivid purple
- **2** 10 mm wood saucer beads, green
- **8** 6º seed beads, metallic copper
- 16 in. (41 cm) 22-gauge wire

ALL PROJECTS

- pair of earring wires
- chainnose and roundnose pliers
- diagonal wire cutters

Tiny bunches

1. For each earring: Cut a 3-in. (7.6 cm) piece of wire. Make a wrapped loop (Basics). String a round bead, a saucer bead, and a round. Make the first half of a wrapped loop.
2. Cut a 3-in. (7.6 cm) piece of chain, beginning and ending with a small link. Attach the end links and the unwrapped loop. Complete the wraps.
3. Open a jump ring (Basics). Attach four 6º seed beads and the center link of the chain. Close the jump ring.
4. Open the loop of an earring wire and attach the dangle. Close the loop.

Stacks

1 For each earring: On a decorative head pin, string an alternating pattern of six 6º seed beads and five round beads. Make a wrapped loop (Basics).
2 Open the loop of an earring wire (Basics) and attach the dangle. Close the loop.

Double Dangles

1 On each wire, string a 6º seed bead and a barrel bead. Make the first half of a wrapped loop (Basics). Attach an end link and complete the wraps.
2 Cut a 1½ -in. (3.8 cm) piece of chain. Cut two 2-in. (5 cm) pieces of wire. On one end of each wire, make a plain loop (Basics).
3 Open the loop of an earring wire. Attach the fourth link of chain and close the loop. Make a second earring the mirror image of the first.

Wire Swirls

1 For each earring: Cut a 3-in. (7.6 cm) piece of wire. On one end, make a plain loop (Basics).
2 String a 6º seed bead, a barrel bead, a saucer bead, and three 6ºs. Make a wrapped loop (Basics).
3 Cut a 5-in. (13 cm) piece of wire. Wrap the wire loosely around the widest part of your roundnose pliers or an 8 mm cylinder. String the wire bead (it should fit over the 6ºs).
4 Open the loop of an earring wire (Basics). Attach the dangle and close the loop.

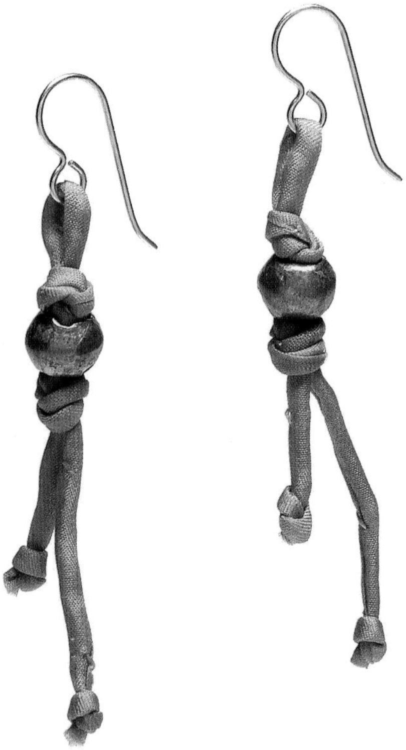

Blend Colors and Textures

designed by Ute Bernsen

SUPPLIES

- 12 in. (30 cm) 2 mm silk strings
- **2** 8–10 mm large-hole beads
- pair of earring wires
- diagonal wire cutters

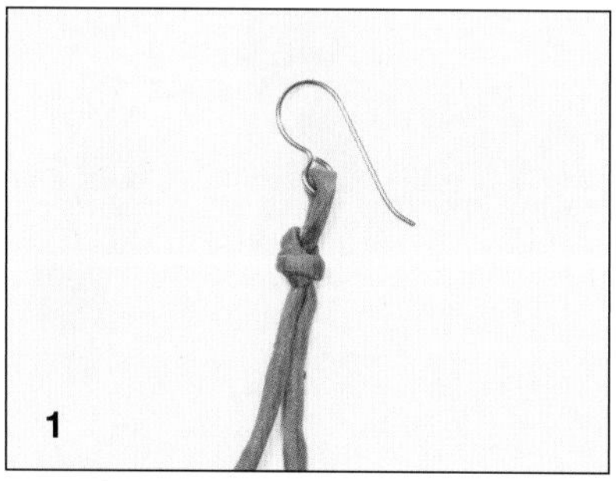

1

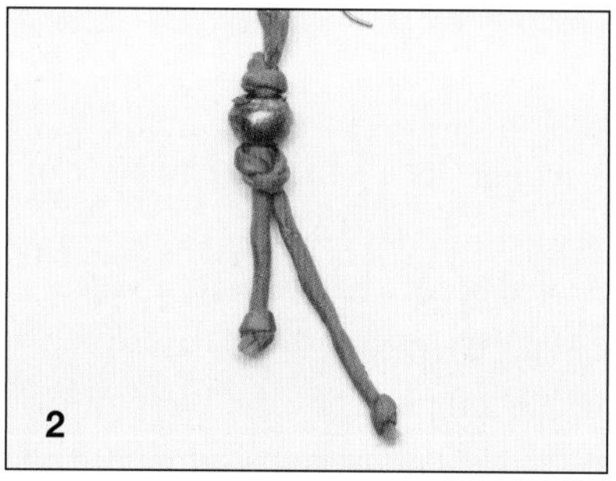

2

1 For each earring: Cut a 6-in. (15 cm) piece of silk string. Center the loop of an earring wire on the string. With both ends, tie an overhand knot (Basics) next to the loop.

2 String a bead over both ends. Tie an overhand knot below the bead. With each end, tie an overhand knot placed asymmetrically. Trim the excess string.

Tip

If you're having trouble stringing the ribbons through the hole of a bead, use a straightened paper clip to push the ends through.

A Blooming Delicacy

designed by Jenny Ross

SUPPLIES

- **2** 30 mm orchid pendants
- **2** 10 mm round beads
- 6 in. (15 cm) 22-gauge wire
- pair of earring wires
- chainnose and roundnose pliers
- diagonal wire cutters

Orchid pendants, dyed jade beads, and clasps from Silver in Style, silverinstyleusa.com.

1 For each earring: Cut a 3-in. (7.6 cm) piece of wire. Make the first half of a wrapped loop (Basics). String a 10 mm bead and make a wrapped loop.

2 Attach the unwrapped loop and the loop of an orchid pendant, and complete the wraps. Open the loop of an earring wire (Basics) and attach the dangle. Close the loop.

A New Focus

Designed by Fernando DaSilva

SUPPLIES

WIRE-WRAPPED EARRINGS

- **2** 25 mm shell donuts
- **2** 12 mm round beads
- **2** 8 mm round pearls
- 16-in. (41 cm) 22-gauge wire
- **2** 2-in. (5 cm) head pins
- **2** 4 mm jump rings
- bentnose or chainnose pliers
- crimping pliers (optional)

BAIL EARRINGS

- **2** 16 mm faceted rondelles
- **2** 8 mm round pearls
- **2** 35 mm oval pinch bails
- **2** 1½-in. (3.8 cm) head pins

BOTH PROJECTS

- pair of lever-back earring wires
- chainnose and roundnose pliers
- diagonal wire cutters

wire-wrapped earrings

1. Make two shell units and two connector units. For each earring: Open the loop of a shell unit (Basics) and attach a loop of a wire-wrapped unit. Close the loop.
2. Use a jump ring to attach the dangle and the loop of an earring wire.

bail earrings

1. Make two pearl units. For each earring: Open the loop of a pearl unit (Basics) and attach the loop of a pinch bail. Close the loop.
2. Open the pinch bail and attach a rondelle. Pinch the bail closed.
3. Open the loop of an earring wire. Attach the dangle and close the loop.

shell unit
On a head pin, string one hole of a shell donut, an 8 mm pearl, and the other hole of the donut. Make a plain loop (Basics).

pearl unit
On a head pin, string an 8 mm pearl and make a plain loop.

connector units

1. Cut an 8-in. (20 cm) piece of 22-gauge wire. At the center of the wire, make a loop. String a round bead. Wrap the wire around the stem once, pull the end above the bead, and wrap once around the stem. Pull the wire down around the bead, wrapping the stem once.
2. Trim the excess wrapping wire below the bead. With the wire above the bead, make a wrapped loop (Basics) perpendicular to the first loop. Use your fingers to make loose wraps above the bead. Trim the excess wire and tuck the ends (Tip).

 Tip

For the wire-wrapped earrings, use crimping pliers to tuck the end of the wire close to the bead.

Short and Chic

designed by Susan Kennedy

SUPPLIES

- **2** 12 mm round large-hole lampworked beads
- **2** 6 mm rondelles
- **2** 6 mm drops
- **2** 1½-in. (3.8 cm) head pins
- **2** 10 mm jump rings
- **4** 7 mm jump rings
- **2** 5 mm jump rings
- pair of earring wires
- chainnose and roundnose pliers
- diagonal wire cutters

1 Open a 7 mm jump ring (Basics). Attach a drop and close the jump ring. Use a 10 mm jump ring to attach a lampworked bead and the drop unit.

2 On a head pin, string a rondelle. Make a wrapped loop (Basics).

3 Use a 7 mm jump ring to attach the rondelle unit to the drop unit.

4 Use a 5 mm jump ring to attach the rondelle unit to an earring wire. Make a second earring the mirror image of the first.

Beautiful by Nature

designed by Jane Konkel

SUPPLIES

- **2** 12 mm enameled flowers
- **2** 13 mm enameled bead caps
- **2** 2-in. (5 cm) decorative head pins
- pair of earring wires
- chainnose and roundnose pliers
- diagonal wire cutters

1. For each earring: On a decorative head pin, string a flower and a bead cap. Bend the head pin up in back of the bead cap. Make the first half of a wrapped loop (Basics).

2. Make two wraps and pull the end down between the flower and bead cap. Make a wrap and trim the excess wire.

3. Open the loop of an earring wire (Basics) and attach the dangle. Close the loop.

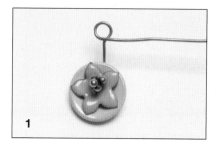

Dream Sequins

designed by Suzanne Branca

SUPPLIES

- **10** 12 mm oval sequins
- **24** 6 mm open-square sequins
- ¾ in. (1.9 cm) rectangle box chain, 3 mm links
- **14** 5 mm jump rings
- pair of lever-back earring wires
- **2** pairs of pliers (may include chainnose, roundnose, or bentnose)
- diagonal wire cutters

Kits for these earrings are available from A Grain of Sand, agrainofsand.com.

1 Open a jump ring (Basics). Attach an open-square sequin, an oval sequin, and a square. Close the jump ring. Make five three-sequin units.

2 Open the jump ring of a three-sequin unit. Attach a square and close the jump ring. Use a jump ring to attach a second square. Cut a two-link piece of chain. Use a jump ring to attach the dangle to the chain.

3 Attach two three-sequin units to each jump ring added in step 2.

4 Open the loop of an earring wire (Basics). Attach the dangle and close the loop. Make a second earring.

Grow Your Collection

designed by Lori Anderson

SUPPLIES

- **2** 19 mm Lucite leaf beads
- **2** 14 mm Lucite flower beads
- **4** 4 mm bicone crystals
- **6** 3 mm flat spacers
- **2** 2-in. (5 cm) head pins
- pair of earring wires
- chainnose and roundnose pliers
- diagonal wire cutters

1 On a head pin, string a bicone crystal, a flower bead, and a leaf bead. Make a right-angle bend in back of the leaf.

2 String three spacers and a bicone. Make a wrapped loop (Basics).

3 Open the loop of an earring wire (Basics). Attach the dangle and close the loop. Make a second earring.

String Art

designed by Arlet Soldevilla

SUPPLIES

- metallic sewing thread
- 10 in. (25 cm) 12-gauge wire
- 8 ft. (2.4 m) 22- or 24-gauge wire
- **2** 6 mm jump rings
- pair of earring wires
- chainnose and roundnose pliers
- diagonal wire cutters
- cylindrical object (like a pill bottle)
- Twist 'n' Curl or Coiling Gizmo coiling tool

1 To make a coil: Hold the handle of the coiling tool in your right hand. String 22- or 24-gauge wire through the hole in the crossbar. Bend the end to stabilize it, and allow the spool to hang freely.

2 Hold the wire against the rod, near the handle. Guide the wire with your left hand while spinning the handle with your right index finger. Remove the coil and pull the ends to slightly separate the coils. Make two 4-in. (10 cm) coils.

3 For each earring: Cut a 5-in. (13 cm) piece of 12-gauge wire. String the coil. Wrap the wire around a cylindrical object to make a teardrop-shaped frame.

4 On one end, trim the wire to ½ in. (1.3 cm). Make a plain loop (Basics) perpendicular to the teardrop.

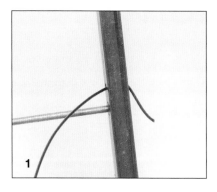

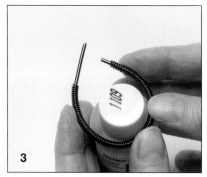

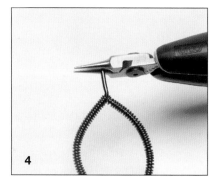

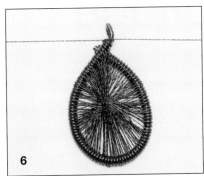

5

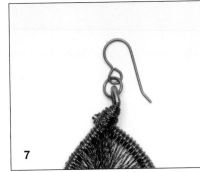

6

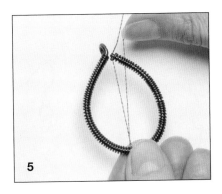

Tip
As you pull the thread between the coils, don't pull the wire too tightly. Otherwise you risk changing the shape of the frame.

7

5 Leaving the thread on the spool, tie a surgeon's knot (Basics) to attach the thread to the top of the frame, leaving a 3-in. (7.6 cm) tail. Wind the thread around the teardrop by pulling it straight to the bottom, between the two center coils. Bring it back up behind the teardrop, between the two coils next to the knot. Bring the thread back down to the coils just to the left of the center ones.

6 Continue winding the thread back and forth between coils, working your way around the entire frame. Tie a surgeon's knot around the stem.

7 Wind both ends of the thread around the stem and tie another surgeon's knot. Trim the excess thread. Open a jump ring (Basics). Attach the dangle and the loop of an earring wire. Close the jump ring.

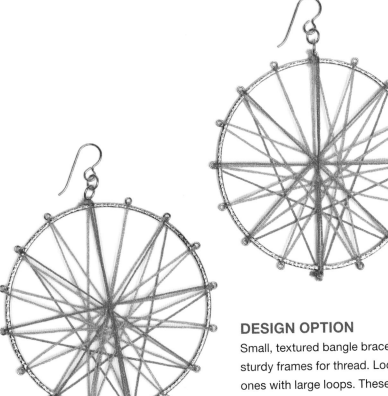

DESIGN OPTION
Small, textured bangle bracelets make sturdy frames for thread. Look for thin ones with large loops. These are from Fusion Beads, fusionbeads.com.

High-Voltage Hues

designed by Jane Konkel

SUPPLIES

- **6** 45 mm shell donuts, in three colors
- **4** 10 mm jump rings
- **8** 6 mm jump rings
- pair of earring wires
- **2** pairs of pliers

1 For each earring: Open a 6 mm jump ring (Basics) and attach a donut. Close the jump ring. Repeat with two more donuts in different colors.

2 Use a 10 mm jump ring to attach each 6 mm jump ring.

3 Use a 6 mm jump ring to attach the dangle and the loop of an earring wire.

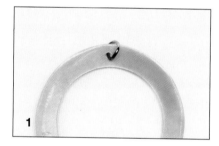

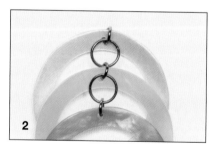

Square Up

designed by Naomi Fujimoto

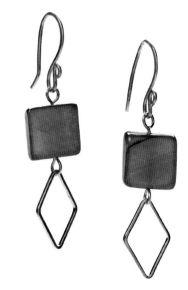

SUPPLIES

- **2** 10 mm square shell beads
- **2** 16 mm diamond-shaped links
- 2½ in. (6.4 cm) 22-gauge wire
- pair of earring wires
- chainnose and roundnose pliers
- diagonal wire cutters

1 For each earring: Cut a 1¼-in. (3.2 cm) piece of wire. Make a plain loop (Basics). String a square bead and make a plain loop perpendicular to the first loop.

2 Open a loop of the bead unit (Basics). Attach a diamond-shaped link and close the loop. Open the loop of an earring wire. Attach the dangle and close the loop.

1

2

Crescents of Color

designed by Jane Konkel

SUPPLIES

CRESCENT EARRINGS

- **2** 38 mm enameled crescents
- 3 in. (7.6 cm) chain, 2 mm links
- **4** 4 mm jump rings
- pair of earring wires

DOUBLE-RECTANGLE EARRINGS

- **2** 38 mm enameled rectangles
- **2** 18 mm enameled rectangles, with two holes
- **2** 6 mm jump rings
- pair of earring wires

SINGLE-RECTANGLE EARRINGS

- **2** 38 mm enameled rectangles
- 3 in. (7.6 cm) chain, 2 mm links
- **2** 6 mm jump rings
- **2** 4 mm jump rings
- pair of lever-back earring wires

ALL PROJECTS

- **2** pairs of pliers
- diagonal wire cutters

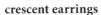

crescent earrings

1 For each earring: Cut a 1½-in. (3.8 cm) piece of chain with an odd number of links. Open the loop of an earring wire (Basics) and attach the center link of chain. Close the loop.

2 On each end, use jump rings to attach a link and a loop of a crescent.

double-rectangle earrings

1 For each earring: Open a jump ring (Basics) and attach a long rectangle and a short rectangle. Close the jump ring.

2 Open the loop of an earring wire and attach the dangle. Close the loop.

single-rectangle earrings

1 For each earring: Cut a 1½-in. (3.8 cm) piece of chain. Open a 6 mm jump ring (Basics) and attach an end link and a rectangle. Close the jump ring.

2 Use a 4 mm jump ring to attach the dangle and the loop of a lever-back earring wire.

contributors

Lori Anderson is the author of *Bead Soup*. Contact her at lori@lorianderson.net.

Carolina Angel Diaz moved to New York City from Colombia over ten years ago. She has been beading ever since and draws inspiration from people and places in the Big Apple. Contact Carolina at cayoyaangel@hotmail.com.

Ute Bernsen is married with two grown children and lives in Carlsbad, Calif. An artist, silk painter, meditation teacher, and jewelry designer, she is creating a course that combines beading or painting with meditation. Contact her at ute@silkpaintingisfun.com.

Heather Boardman is a glass artist and jewelry designer focusing her work on bright, fun colors and interesting shapes. Contact her via email at heather@hmbstudios.com, or visit her website, hmbstudios.etsy.com.

Suzanne Branca owns A Grain of Sand, a Web-based store that sells vintage and contemporary beads and findings. When she's not playing with beads, she loves to play with her grandbaby, Jaxon. Contact Suzanne at suzanne@agrainofsand.com or visit agrainofsand.com.

Ashley Bunting is a jewelry designer based in Portland, Maine. She is a brand ambassador for Xuron Tools and runs her independent jewelry business, Miss Ashley Kate. Contact her at missashleykate@gmail.com.

Christianne Camera started making jewelry as a hobby, but she and her sister, Maria, turned that hobby into a business, Bella! Bella! Visit their Facebook page at facebook.com/bellabellajewelry, or contact Christianne in care of Kalmbach Books.

Felicia Cantillo can be contacted at feliciacantillo@hotmail.com or by visiting feliciacantillo.com.

Laurie-Anne Clinton is a jewelry artist from Toronto, Canada. She is married and has five "adoring and adorable" cats. She loves working with glass, vintage Lucite, and mixed metals. Contact her at flirt@flirtdesigns.ca.

Ann Cook is a jewelry designer and teacher from Milwaukee, Wis. Contact her at acookc@earthlink.net.

Candie Cooper has been beading since the eighth grade. She is the author of Felted Jewelry and Metalworking 101 for Beaders and lives with Rocker, her corgi/long-haired Chihuahua mix. Contact Candie via candiecooper.com.

Fernando DaSilva is a designer and the product development and creative manager for John Bead. He's also the author of Lovely Knots: An Introduction to Chinese Knotting, available from John Bead, johnbead.com for stores. Contact Fernando at fernando.dasilva@johnbead.com or visit dasilvajewelry.com.

Contact **Mary Delaney** in care of Kalmbach Books.

Anna Elizabeth Draeger is a well-known jewelry designer, former associate editor for *Bead&Button* magazine, and the author of *Crystal Brilliance*, *Great Designs for Shaped Beads*, and *Crystal Play*. Her website is originaldesignsbyanna.squarespace.com.

Lorelei Eurto has been creating beaded jewelry since 2007. Contact Lorelei at ljeurto@gmail.com or visit loreleieurtojewelry.com.

Naomi Fujimoto is editor of *Bead Style* magazine and author of *Cool Jewels: Beading Projects for Teens*. Visit her at cooljewelsbynaomi.etsy.com, or contact her in care of *Bead Style*.

Miriam Fuld lives in Israel with her husband, four children, and their black Cocker-Pinscher. Contact Miriam at mim@mimzdesign.com or visit mimzdesign.com.

Karen Galbraith can be contacted via her website, jumpingjunebug.com.

Allyson Giesen can be contacted at beadingdreams@gmail.com or by visiting beadingdreams.com.

Monica Han is an award-winning mixed-media jewelry designer and teacher in Potomac, Md. Contact her via email at mhan@dreambeads.biz.

Leah Hanoud has been beading for more than 15 years. Contact Leah at turq2000@turquoise-stringbeads.com or visit turquoise-stringbeads.com.

Beth Haywood has been beading for years and loving every sparkly minute of it. "I'm a magpie at heart," she says. Contact her via email at beth.heywood@gmail.com, or visit her blog, themermaidsden.blogspot.com.

Kristina Henning works for a nonprofit that helps families of children with disabilities in the education system by day, but by night she creates beautiful gemstone jewelry while keeping an eye on her son, a dog, and a herd of rescue cats. Contact Kristina at info@kristinahenning.com or visit kristinahenning.com.

Cathy Jakicic is the author of the books *Jewelry Projects from a Beading Insider* and *Hip Handmade Memory Jewelry*, and is the former editor of *Bead Style* magazine. Contact her via email at cathyjakicic@att.net.

Brightly colored stones are **Meredith Jensen's** beading material of choice. Contact Meredith via her website, m-jewelry.net.

Karen Karon can be contacted via her website, karenkaron.com.

Susan Kennedy makes glass beads in her home studio in Pittsburgh, Pa. To see more of her work, visit her website at sue@suebeads.com or contact her at sue@suebeads.com.

Jane Konkel is a former associate editor of *Bead Style* magazine. Contact her in care of Kalmbach Books.

Sonia Kumar doesn't have a bead store near her home, but she gets by with a little help from her friends. They give her old jewelry and she makes the pieces into something new. Contact Sonia at soniakumar92@yahoo.com or visit catchalljewelry.etsy.com.

Kelsey Lawler is assistant editor for *Bead Style* magazine. Contact her at klawler@beadstylemag.com.

Monica Lueder is a big fan of crystals. She lives and creates in Cedarburg, Wis. Contact her at mdesign@wi.rr.com.

Becky Machinski can be contacted at becky@silversilkonline.com or by visiting silversilkonline.com.

Irina Miech is an artist, teacher, and the author of more than books on jewelry making. She also oversees her retail bead supply business and classroom studio, Eclectica and The Bead Studio, in Brookfield, Wis. Contact Irina at Eclectica, 262-641-0910, or via email at eclecticainfo@sbcglobal.net.

Contact **Denise Yezbak Moore** in care of Kalmbach Books.

Contact **Sandy Parpart** at sandyparpart@sbcglobal.net.

Contact **Glenda Paunonen** at info@beadsgonewild.com or visit beadsgonewild.com.

Dee Perry is a jewelry designer and bead store owner (Bead Need) from Davie, Fla. She has also created the Claspon-Claspoff line of clasps and components. Contact Dee at info@claspon-claspoff.com or visit claspon-claspoff.com.

Madelin Adriani Pratama lives with her husband and two sons in Jakarta, Indonesia. Contact Maddie at madelinadriani@hotmail.com or visit facebook.com/illuminatijuwel.

Leslie Rogalski is an artist, jewelry designer, and author. She lives with her husband in Haverton, Pa., and has a daughter studying musical theater. Contact Leslie at leslierogalski@gmail.com or visit leslierogalski.com.

Jenny Ross started selling her jewelry at local street fairs and now works as a wholesale importer of precious metals. Contact Jenny via her website, silverinstyleusa.com.

Arlet Flores Soldevilla was *Bead Style's* Rising Star in the July 2012 issue. Contact Arlet at arletofs@yahoo.com or visit kenasstones.com.

Contact **Jessica Tiemens** in care of Kalmbach Books.

Liisa Turunen works at Crystal Creations Bead Institute in West Palm Beach, Fla. She lives with her husband, four cats, and a dog and is inspired by her mother, the owner of Crystal Creations Bead Institute. Contact Liisa at info@beadsgonewild.com or visit beadsgonewild.com.

Jenny Van loves shopping at gem and bead shows. When she's not making jewelry, she enjoys watching Korean movies and TV dramas like Bones. Contact Jenny at jenny@beadsj.com or visit beadsj.com.

Kimberly Wayne lives in New Berlin, Wis., with her two dogs, Mya and Layla. She works at Eclectica bead store in Brookfield, Wis., and also does freelance interior design. Contact Kimberly at theb1onde@hotmail.com.

Ann Westby started making jewelry in 2001 and quickly discovered she had a passion for wirework. She can be contacted via her website, annwestby.com.

Diane Whiting is the author of *Convertible Crystal Jewelry*, and her work has been featured in magazines and books. Contact Diane at dwhitingdesigns@cox.net, or visit www.dianewhitingdesigns.com.

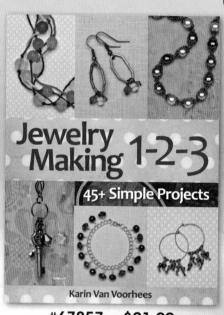